Books written previously by the same author:

'Our Birth on Earth'

'When Scorpio Ruled the World'

'Heaven's Message – How to Read it Nowadays'

'Character Portraits of England's Plantagenet Kings'

'Concise Character Portraits of England's Tudor, Stuart and Protectorate Rulers'

'Character Portraits of England's Germanic Monarchs'

'**Simply Now** – Our Simple A.D. 2020 Situation'

'**Simply Now 2** – Personality and Love'

SIMPLY
NOW 3
OUR INDIVIDUAL FUTURES

CHRIS STUBBS

Order this book online at www.trafford.com
or email orders@trafford.com

Most Trafford titles are also available at major online book retailers.

Print information available on the last page.

ISBN: 978-1-6987-0067-0 (sc)
ISBN: 978-1-6987-0068-7 (e)

Library of Congress Control Number: 2020906984

Trafford rev. 04/17/2020

www.trafford.com
North America & international
toll-free: 1 888 232 4444 (USA & Canada)
fax: 812 355 4082

CONTENTS

ACKNOWLEDGEMENTS

To the memories of A. Leo, R.C. Davison and M.E. Hone, all of whom were senior officers of the Astrological Association.

We are very grateful to the parents of Oliver Strate for permitting his use, as our example of Forwards Astrology. As requested, we have disguised his identity, and have not revealed his natal data. He is their second son, of a single and natural birth. His Ideal Birth Time was within minutes of the natural one.

FOREWORD

When clients ask an astrologer to 'do' their horoscopes, almost always the clients want to know what their futures hold, and why not? As a result, we have tried to work through what needs to be done to produce a relevant set of predictions for a client, if at all.

Firstly, we needed to produce a client's Character Portrait, which is the indispensable starting point for any further 'synastry' or 'prediction' exercise for the client. We have carried out two exercises of 'backwards astrology' on well-known people, from their biographies and their natural birth data. From the former, we obtained dates and times of important life-events, and from the latter, their character portraits. The two people we have chosen are Queen Mary of Teck (QM) [wife of the UK's King George V] and Gerald Ford, the 38th President of the U.S.A. (PF).

In the past, four, main 'methods of prediction' have been proposed. We applied all four to QM's major life-events, and found that one method was the most likely, but another was still possible. Then we applied these two methods to PF's life-events, and found that the most likely one was still the best. This method uses a combination of Secondary Progressions and Transits, is the most popular, and is our 'method of choice'.

Then we carried out an exercise of 'forwards astrology' from the acceptable, natural, birth data for a boy, Oliver. From this we produced his Character Portrait, and have determined his predictions, using the 'method of choice', for the ends of the separate and successive cycles of his progressed Moon. Will it be possible to see how these predictions tally with his life-events? Perhaps only time will tell!

CHAPTER 1

The Composition of a Human Life

"The Name of the Game is Astrology"

A century ago, the main value of Astrology consisted of describing the chief events of a life, so that they may have been known beforehand. This is the 'fatalistic' approach. Alternatively, the 'free-will' approach is based on the motto: "Man know thyself" (mainly as an individual). The rule here is based upon the idea that: 'the stars and the planets only incline, they do not compel'. Nowadays, it would seem that the truth lies somewhere between these two alternatives.

More than one hundred years ago, Alan Leo prefaced all his interpretations of 'directions'; sent to clients by:-

"You will greatly assist our scientific work, and enable us to check inaccuracies, if you will inform us, at the end of the period for which 'directions' have been calculated, of the actual result of your experiences (if any), when the events predicted do (or not) coincide with the 'directions' given".

Today, we could use such an approach, which is an example of "backwards" astrology (see later). As a result of the responses obtained, Leo adopted the system involving the "Progressed Horoscope" as the centre for determining the successive events of life, i.e. 'prediction', but admitted that this system, although simply the most satisfactory available, was not ideal. He limited his approach to those who were neither too young, nor too old, i.e. either not mature, or not flexible, enough. Additionally, some persons were more capable of responding to, or were more sensitive to, 'heavenly influences', than others. He asked the question: "Why are lives so strongly different?" Some seemed to be fated to be born rich and happy, while others became poor and miserable; some possessing stable humour and clear intellect, while others were fools and idiots. And again: "Was life merely a matter of chance?"

The question of Fate versus Free-Will has exercised the minds of many seekers of truth throughout the ages. "As ye sow, so shall ye reap" is an axiom followed by many people. However, there is no real evidence to suggest that any actions in the past affect our futures, unless we allow this to happen consciously. There is the principle of the mind being superior to nature, through which we are capable of surpassing the order and system (fate) of the World [Iamblicus]. By exercising the spiritual faculties of his mind, man can at any, and at all times, lift himself above the ever changing plane of the planets. This is the true making of one's own future, and the solution to the problem of fatalism.

Alan Leo believed that Astrology alone could provide clear and definite answers to his questions. He concluded that Environment, Heredity and Character comprised the three great factors in human destiny, the understanding of which clarified the problem of fate, and provided us with ways to escape from its bondage. We all needed to find out not merely the 'How of life, but also the Why!' In addition, none of us has any choice over our early environments, perhaps they are prepared for us (or we for them?) and so environment becomes our destiny; but also many of us alter and shape our environment, and so are no longer ruled by it.

'Character' is different in all human beings. Some seem to born 'bad', and no amount of moral, or mental, training alters, or improves, them. They tend to go from 'bad' to 'worse', cursed from birth by poor heredity, wretched environment and everything conducing, apparently, to draw out the very worst, and the most evil, part of their natures. Leo asked: "What explanation do we get from our moral and religious teachers regarding these disparate characters?" "Why is one person pure, and another the opposite?" Astrology throws some light on the answer to this latter question. It points to the planets (stars?) as the cause for the events of life, which follow after human birth. The three factors, namely, Environment, Heredity and Character seem to exercise their influence as follows:-

1. Environment provides conditions for expression of the latent qualities inherent in a person.
2. Heredity supplies the vessel – the functional, or faculty, according to that person's ancestry, and

3. Character, which is the inherent quality of that person, which is brought with that person, and is 'the root of merit', which is either susceptible to its environment, or rises above, dominates and changes it. In this particular sense 'Character becomes Destiny'.

For example, in the growth of young children, certain traits of character, not wholly accounted for by heredity, or environment, arise as they develop. Many children of the same family, even when all have become distinguished, have become famous/notorious, for their great differences in character. Nevertheless, it would seem that, as the main factor contributing to destiny, character plays the prominent part. Everyone is either strong or weak, good or evil, pronounced or indifferent. Within every character there is a 'will' that may be weak or strong, according to 'temperament'. Those who study human nature become aware of the complicated nature of character. We could say that human beings manifest themselves through a) temperament, b) feelings and emotions, c) mental expressions and d) through phases of thought.

Our own physical bodies are of a certain temperament, upon which character is mainly dependent. Thus, a person possessing a <u>vital</u> temperament will not fit easily into a hard environment because he/she will love and desire ease. Through this temperament the feelings and emotions affect destiny. Those of the <u>mental</u> temperament, living in the mind, will be affected more by 'mental' rather than 'material' conditions. However, those with the <u>motive</u> temperament incline towards power, organisation and force. Hence each temperament can affect its surroundings according to the strength of character, or will, that lies behind it. Also, apparently, each of us is surrounded by an 'aura' that is composed, at least in part, of his/her thoughts, feelings and emotions, and this is a part of that person from the moment of birth onwards. We can conclude that character seems very complicated, and so destiny will be a difficult matter to interpret.

Matter is fated to assume shape and form, but the life within that form is destined to control it, sooner or later. Yet we can claim self-evidently that all living creatures are basically identical in spirit and in <u>essence</u> (a part of Simply Now?) Yet they differ in manifestation, according to the matter in which they are clothed, and in their attitude towards their own being. All the different ways of manifestation can be described through the charts of Epoch and Birth constructed from the interpretations of the positions of the Sun, Moon, Morin Point and planets within them, as well as finally, from 'Directions'.

The Three Cycles.

In a full, human life, the Moon (concerned with all psychic changes) makes three complete revolutions by <u>progressive</u> (each day stands for one year, see later) <u>motion</u> around the circle of the horoscope.

The first of these three lunar cycles, lasting for about 28 years (or roughly the same time as the duration of one of Saturn's orbits around the Sun) corresponds to the physical body. Normally, attention is centred on physical actions in this cycle. It decides the question of passion or purity; bondage or freedom; hell or heaven.

The second cycle, from about 28 to 56 years, corresponds to the Moon specifically. The psychic nature is expanded, the emotions become more refined, controlled and the person grows towards 'the light', except in a few cases, where the downward, or reverse path, has been chosen.

The third cycle, up to 84 years, (or roughly the same time as the duration of one of Uranus's orbits around the Sun) brings intuition, wisdom and the spiritual side of life. This has been called the cycle of reason and gives 'the years of the philosophical mind'.

These three cycles are also correlated with the twelve, seven year cycles (c.f. in Shakespeare's "As you like it", we find the seven ages of man); four for the body and action, four for the mind and emotions, and finally, four for knowledge and consciousness. The whole of them interact to evolve the sevenfold and twelvefold man.

— — — — — — — — — — — — — — — — — — — —

CHAPTER 2

Our Physical Composition and Our Character

"The Name of the Game is DNA and the Name of the Game is Life"

Probably, the Earth – Moon binary system formed some 4.5 billion years ago as the result of a large collision between the original (proto) Earth and a Mars sized body, Theia, having an orbit around the Sun, similar to that of proto-Earth. We think that this collision occurred on the off-side (from the Sun) of proto-Earth, causing the resulting proto-Earth – Theia combination to spin around on its axis once every six hours (a short day), in the direction that it still does. The resulting Moon was ejected roughly into the plane of the Solar-System (i.e. the ecliptic) in the direction around the New-Earth that it does now, but then only about five thousand miles away from it. The gravitational pull of the newly-created Moon upon the New-Earth then, would have been far stronger (<u>ca.</u> times 1600) than it is now. This pull could have initiated the start of Life chemistry that would then have led to the appearance of Life-on-Earth, but not in the same way on Mars, which lacks a suitable satellite.

Life on New-Earth began relatively very soon after the creation of the Earth – Moon binary system (within some 700,000 years). We know that life has left traces of its existence here for at least 3.8 billion years. Life chemical compounds produced on the Earth, show optical activity, i.e. their solutions in water rotate the plane of polarised light passing through them almost always to the left, and so only rarely to the right. The biochemical processes producing them probably depended on the specific direction of the Moon's passing around the Earth, coupled with the particular direction of the Earth's daily spin on its axis. Thus, the ability of life chemical compounds to rotate the plane of polarised light (demonstrated over a century ago) points to their Earthly origin, rather than to that in outer-space. Without the Moon, and so without its role in generating life and birth processes, it appears that Life-on-Earth would never have formed, as it did.

Additionally, the newly formed binary Earth – Moon system would have been more stable than if proto-Earth had continued to exist by itself, without colliding with Theia. We explain the fact that the Moon's core is relatively small compared with that of the present Earth, because the off-side collision caused it to consist more of proto-Earth's and Theia's crusts than of their central cores.

Any criterion for the existence of evolved life as it is today, constitutes a Prime Cause. Apart from the possible need for the Moon's strong gravitational pull, there are other Prime Causes for life's evolution on Earth, e.g. 1) the need for the Sun's heat and light; 2) the availability of water over most of the Earth's temperate surface; 3) liquid water being more dense than its frozen, solid form, ice (this is rare) so that it freezes from the top down, thereby enabling life to continue to function in the cold, liquid water beneath; 4) the source of warmth from the Earth's core; 5) the presence of chemical elements essential for life, such as carbon, hydrogen, sulphur, nitrogen, phosphorus and oxygen later, as well as 6) mutations.

The billions of years that have elapsed since the Earth first held life, comprise the "deep-time" of joint biological evolution and geological change. Compared with "deep-time", all of human time seems but a passing few moments. We are very familiar with geological change from television documentaries showing grinding tectonic plates, accompanying earthquakes, volcanoes, landslides and tsunamis that rush across our oceans. Moreover, we must not forget the more usual ravages of fire, storm, tide and wind, all of which contribute to massive geological change. By contrast, biological development (fertilised cells -> baby, etc.), if not evolution, requires more calm, controlled, stable and safe conditions in order to flourish.

We can visualise the Earth as a bio-sphere covered with a thin skin of tissue, called life. Living things are composed of invisible, soft building blocks called cells, every one of which carries within itself a singular, chemical compound (molecule) called deoxyribonucleic acid (DNA), made up from just five chemical elements, just mentioned, but with the omission of sulphur. It borders on the incredible that a life-chemical compound, as complicated as DNA, has managed to evolve and replicate in the way that it does, and did. Our minds have struggled for decades trying to comprehend all that it has, and is, doing.

DNA unites all of life on Earth in a common history because every cell of every living thing has contained a version of DNA for a billion years. Because DNA can replicate itself, living things can produce off-spring, and so possess a common descent from shared ancestors. The breath-taking idea that a single DNA life-form was the ancestor (LUCA stands for the Last Universal Common Ancestor) of all living things, spawns a sort of "Big-Birth" theory.

The growth of cells from a fertilised egg into a living creature is called 'development', and the development of life on Earth is called 'evolution'. Both development and evolution bring about structures of amazing complexity that are time-dependent and structured hierarchically, from the interaction of genes (composed entirely of DNA) with proteins. Not only do we derive our physical form, but also our characters from our genes. The DNA in every cell of a person – called that person's genome – is very like an encyclopaedia in design and content. We ourselves are very big compared with a cell, and cells are very big compared with the atoms of the chemical elements from which they, and so we, are made. We are composed of one hundred trillion (million, million) cells and each cell is made up of one hundred trillion atoms. Thus, the complexity of a cell in atomic terms, is about as complex as the complexity of a person (brain included) in cellular terms.

Interestingly, 99.6% of our working DNA (only a fraction of the total) is just the same as that of a chimpanzee. That residual 0.4% of a part, suddenly seems remarkably important.

Mutations are rare, but beneficial ones, since life is old, are the underlying cause of life's diversity. Without mutations, life would have died out long ago from its failure to adapt to fluctuations in temperature, atmosphere and water level. Hence mutations constitute a Prime Cause. With slight but continuous mutation, the descendants of some creatures have been able to survive myriad, environmental disturbances to become the millions of different species that we recognise today.

Looking at the present richness of life on Earth, it is difficult to believe that natural selection, that permits the survival of some, but not all, randomly occurring sequence differences in DNA, is responsible for so many different forms. But every mutation corresponds to a new form, and each mutation must make sense in its own context, before it can serve as the new baseline for the next mutation. In this way, a series of changes (directed chance) will accumulate over time, which will be seen with hindsight, but only with hindsight, as a remarkable parody of an intelligent plan. DNA's wasteful, but so far successful, strategy for surviving environmental stress and competition, through imperfect replication, drives Darwinian natural selection. For us, the rarity of general mutations means that, for all practical purposes, the DNA of our first, fertilised egg-cell, and that of all the cells of the resulting new-born baby, not to mention all the cells of the fully-mature adult, will be identical. This means that we have to work with what we have got, i.e. to build on strengths, guard against weaknesses (rather than try to eliminate them) and so reinforce our own personal judgement. It also means that the usefulness of methods designed to change our personalities, such as brain-washing, must be called into question. The whole of the content of this chapter 2 constitutes a significant and substantial part of 'Simply Now'.

— — — — — — — — — — — — — — — — — — —

CHAPTER 3

The Development of Prediction

"For life, the Earth is the Centre of the Universe"

Man is certainly affected by the Heavens, and in turn, is able to act upon the results. Astrology is the science of subtle relationships that cannot be interpreted easily in terms of physical science, and cannot even be brought readily within the conception, fundamental in physics, of causation. Similarly also, psychic phenomena cannot be explained in terms of the physical sciences. On the other hand, Astrology does not constitute an Art by which the future can be foretold in detail. This would constitute fortune telling. Any remark on the possibilities for the future, should be preceded by the phrase: "The likelihood is that . . ." and should be understood to be the probable outcome of the development of the potentialities shown by the two natal charts of Epoch and Birth, and as conditions of life, not as of precise events. Dates given are approximate, but are calculated as exactly as possible from the person's natal charts. Although they may point to events, their main use is intended to be as a guide to what type of helpful activity, or lack of it, is to be stressed for that time. Astrology attempts to indicate a life pattern, but there are more ways than one, in which this can be worked out.

Both astrologers and their clients accept the use of the word "Progressions" to cover all calculations pertaining to trends in a life for any specified time. The word, in conjunction with "Transits", applies only to the movement of the planets in their cycles, by which the potentialities, shown in natal charts, may be expected to develop. "Transits" to natal positions are regarded as more important generally than those to "progressed" places. The effect of transits is most noticeable when they act as a stimulation to a coincident 'progression'. This phenomenon of excitation, which is one of the most useful and exact in Astrology, may be stated as a law, thus:

"If, at the time that a 'progressed' body is in aspect to another by direction, either of these bodies forms an aspect by transit with either of

the two 'direction' bodies, then the 'transit' will excite the 'direction' into immediate operation."

Any other transiting body would not act as an excitement. This law may enable the astrologer to determine, even within a day, when a 'direction' will operate. Student astrologers, who find that one 'transit' acts with great power, while another with very little, will find this explained by the fact that the first 'transit' sparks to ignite a 'direction', while the second just sparks it.

It is not too difficult to do astrology 'backwards', and this proves to be very helpful later, when trying to do it 'forwards'.

The planetary configurations subsequent to epoch, or birth, produce results in the life according to a time measure of one day equals a year. A Day for a Year is the phrase generally used in reference to the way in which astrological 'progressions' are worked. This system of progressions correlates with the orbital movement of the planets with respect to the Earth, one day's movement after epoch/birth corresponding to one year's development of growing life. No scientist has yet explained how it is that the life of every human being on this Earth is geared to its two cyclic movements, i.e. its daily rotation on its own central axis plus its yearly revolution around the Sun itself. Astrologers believe that this is a fact, but they cannot explain it. On first thought, note that there seems little justification for Astrologers' intuition that we can use the day-for-a-year assumption, when calculating 'progressions' and subsequent 'predictions' from them (but see statistical studies, later). Yet it remains the basis for the working of progressions, or directions (and transits) by what is known as the Secondary System. This name differentiates it from the Primary System, which correlates with the rotational movement of the Earth itself, i.e. the passage of 1^0 of right ascension over the Meridian, being equated with one year of life. Its accuracy depends on knowing the precise moment of the Epoch/Birth, as well as having the correct House system for determining intermediate House cusps/ centres. [However, use of the Morinus House system, coupled with the Pre-Natal Epoch could provide a straightforward basis for using the Primary System].

In addition, some astrologers have expressed the view that Secondary directions are unsatisfactory because they do not always furnish appropriate aspects to account for the various events of life. On the other hand, those who combine Secondary directions with transits, usually regard the former as arising solely from natal charts, and the latter as being completely external to a person's horoscope, representing the general conditions in the outside World. However, Davison extended the Day for a year assumption to include Day for a Day 'progressions', i.e. 'transits' themselves. Hence, in this way, 'transits' become an integral part of Secondary directions, being a logical extension and development of the basic idea underlying the system.

Because time always proceeds forwards, and never backwards, the justification for requiring that planetary positions before the day of epoch/birth have an important bearing on the life of a person, seems poor. The natal charts themselves (of Epoch and Birth) represent a definite charge of power, at a particular moment, for a person. The angles of a chart are points in space only, and serve us by specifying the Earth's orientation with the Solar System at the particular moments of the person's Epoch and Birth. Also, they are important for determining a chart's rulers, as well as for specifying the intermediate House centres, but their influence generally, for our futures, must surely be negligible when compared with that of the planets.

To summarise: the main features of the system of Secondary Directions comprise:

1. One single unit, the mean Solar Day, can be equated not only to a year, but also to a day. But it can also be equated to the time of the Moon's orbit around the Earth (month).
2. As a first approximation, 'progressions' are valid when measured 'forward' only.
3. The angles of natal charts rotate at a rate equal to the Sun's progress through the Zodiac/ecliptic. Again, as a first approximation, these positions are of relatively minor importance in determining the timing of events, and of their natures.

An Alternative Method for Determining
our Individual Futures

Addey has discussed some of the various applications of harmonics in natal charts but has made no reference to harmonics as they appear in relation to the unfoldment of these natal charts through progressions, transits and the like. However, it would be very surprising if a principle, which applied overall in the one case, did not apply equally in the other. On the other hand, the work on harmonics has not proved to be transferable readily to interpreting natal charts for individuals, which we should keep in mind.

First of all, Addey asked us to think about what happens when the events of life (indicated by directions) unfold. The course of life is not chaotic, and although some events may appear to happen 'out-of-the-blue', really we are always dealing with orderly sequences of experience. For example, a man may have a period when he is feeling the pinch financially, which leads him to seek promotion, or a better paid job, and this again, if he succeeds, brings new responsibilities and adjustments. Also, it brings a new prosperity that may enable him to put a deposit down on a house. On a different level, a child may have a rather sluggish period of poor health, which makes her vulnerable to infections at school, so that she catches measles, but after a quick recovery, she suddenly blossoms out, bursting with life and energy. It is as if the fever had had a cathartic effect. Or again, at the original level, the corresponding first stage of such an experience, may have been something resembling a nervous breakdown, when life seems to confront a person with an overwhelming dilemma, which he does not know how to deal with; but such situations become resolved sometimes almost imperceptibly; some symbolic act, or experience that happens almost unobserved, releases the tension; suddenly the dilemma abates, equilibrium becomes restored, and confidence is regained.

Now when these experiences are recalled, what is it that is actually remembered? In the last case, it is the dreadful experience of a nervous breakdown, and it is that event that is looked for in 'progressions'. The child's mother, remembers the time when her daughter was so ill with measles that she looks for that event, forgetting the earlier period of poor health, and perhaps does not associate the measles with her daughter's renewed energies. On the other hand, the daughter looks back to the time when she took on a new lease of life and did much better at school, whereas the man who suddenly stepped up in the World, may now regard his promotion as the natural culmination of much effort (and long overdue anyway!) and remembers chiefly the day when he and his wife could at last afford a house of their own. All this goes to show that the course of our lives is not so much a series of isolated events, but rather a flowing sequence of unfoldment, and whereas one person will focus on one stage of the sequence, another will see a different stage as the important event.

In terms of 'progressions', it would seem that as 'progressed' aspects form, we can often relate the sequence of stages to the applying, exact and separating stages of an aspect. In Diagram 1, if we think of planet A forming a 'progressed' aspect with planet B, point x may represent stage 1 (the 'hardship' period of the man, the little girl's poor health, or the nervous breakdown of our last example; y may indicate stage 2 (promotion, the measles, or the unnoticed resolution of conflict) and point z will show the consequent improvement (the new house, the fresh energy at school, or confidence restored).

Diagram 1 :-

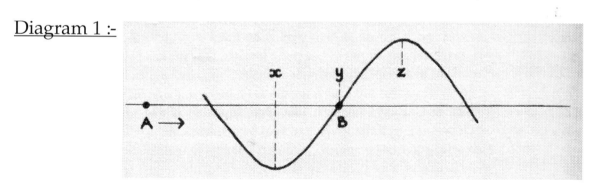

The period from x -> y and from y -> z may be a month, say, or a fortnight, or two years. In each case the process is the development of one principle, or type of aspect, through various stages; in the first case a Saturn (planet B with the Moon as planet A) aspect is at work; x = Saturn denied (penury); y = Saturn resurgent (promotion, responsibility), and z = Saturn enjoyed (acquired bricks and mortar). In the case of the young lady with measles, probably planet B is Mars, and perhaps planet A is the Sun, for hers is a Mars type experience. x = Mars denied (impurities clog the system and the fires of life burn poorly), y = Mars resurgent (cathartic fever) and z = Mars released (the energies burn brightly again). And so on. Notice that in each case, y is a nodal event with a distinct before and after, and that the nodal event itself (promotion, measles) is often short and sharp, in contrast to the before and after stages.

The suggestion is that it is not always the applying aspect that is denied, or repression of the planetary principle involved, sometimes the excess comes first, and the deficiency follows after the aspect. In fact, the four possibilities of Diagram 2 apply. It then becomes a question of what stages of experience we are passing through.

<u>Diagrams 2</u> :-

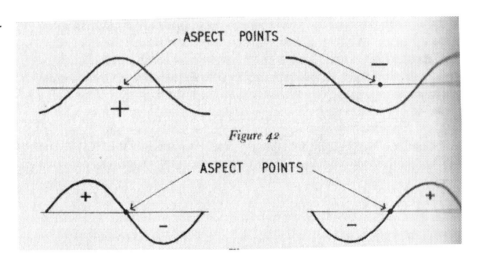

Figure 42

This brings us to the point that we have been leading up to. The different principles and forces at work in life are constantly moving between polarities of positive and negative, full and empty, tension and release, and this is the reason why the notion of 'progressed' aspects, which suddenly pop up from time to time, and then are done with, probably is a false one. As a 'progressed' planet A moves around the circle forming an ever changing relationship with natal planet B, we are always dealing with a regular flux between positive and negative poles of experience. If the gentleman, who was feeling the financial squeeze, and so looking for promotion, thinks that he is going to feel rich forever, then he has got another think coming. But probably he knows, as well as we do, that in a year or two's time, he will be feeling poor again. If he knows of Parkinson's laws, then he will know that expenditure expands to meet income. If he is of a philosophical mind, then he will know that the rhythm moves on.

Actually, we need to think less about exact aspect points and more about the ebb and flow of progressed motions, by trying to determine the types of life rhythms related to different planetary relationships in the 'progressed' chart – for it will seem to be the coincidence of these rhythms at certain intervals that brings the most significant situations, and that these do not always coincide with the conventional aspect points. (Biorhythms footnote?)

But now, let us look at some practice and ask ourselves, for example: "What 'progressions' should we look for at the time of marriage?" and, "Just what are we to look for?" Of course, textbooks have rather a simple approach to such questions, and in this case, have suggested that the 'progressed' Sun, in aspect to a natal Venus, is important. But in fact, the positions of the 'progressed' Sun, in relation to the natal Venus (at the time of marriage in 116 cases of flat-race jockeys) is just the normal, expected distribution relationship of Sun and Venus, and there is no suggestion that Sun in aspect to Venus, as detailed, coincides with marriage.

However, the point about marriage is that it is <u>permanent</u>, a <u>definite</u>, formal agreement <u>binding</u> upon both parties. It introduces an element of <u>stability</u> into their lives and confers a measure of <u>security</u> of relationship and affection. In the past, the woman gained some <u>financial</u> security, and the man <u>financial</u> responsibility. The connection between Venus and money has been well-brought out in Astrology.

Hence, there is no need to go any further, all of this that we have just said, points to a Venus – Saturn relationship. The cases of young men, or women, who have been rather wild in youth, suddenly becoming steadier, more serious and responsible, at the time of marriage, is a commonplace. Saturn is not exalted in Libra for nothing, and this is the time when one's affections crystallise upon one person.

Thus, if there is any sense to be made of planetary relationships, then there <u>must</u> be a characteristic Venus – Saturn relationship of <u>some</u> kind involved here. The usual day-for-a-year method of 'progressions' is well-attested and certainly justifies examination, but symbolic measures, such as the One-Degree (= one year) may be relevant. Either of these may answer our question of: "What is the relationship of 'progressed' Venus to Saturn (for data, we are measuring from the slower planet to the faster) at the time of marriage?" The results of the rather thinly-spread 116 cases of men of a similar type (flat-race jockeys) were enhanced by a collapsing technique from 360^0 to 30^0 and showed a 1st harmonic (conjunction; amp > 10%) near the point of aspect; a 15^0, 2nd harmonic (opposition; amp 35%) and a 6^0, 5th harmonic (quintile; amp 33%). These results are general (and do not apply to women) and the sample is small. But the results did show that there seems to be a typically Saturn – Venus astrological relationship at the time of marriage. Even the One-Degree measure, the 6^0 (quintile relationship) held-up, and also showed a strong 6^0 (quintile) rhythm. Addey suggested that for both 6^0 cases, a five year cycle would fit better during a relatively short age span for marriage.

What then, of transits? Evidently, the same sort of principles apply. The death of a parent is an important psychological event for most people, and this must be enhanced in the case of only sons, and even more so when the event marks the inheritance of lands, title and wealth (with their accompanying responsibilities). W. H. Somerford extracted all cases of only sons where the date of death of the father, and the date of birth of the only son were given, and so the age of inheritance (205 cases), from Burke's Peerage, Baronetage and Knightage, (103rd Ed., 1963.) Somerford provided the natal, progressed and transiting positions of the Sun at the time of inheritance, and the position of the lunation preceding the event (a lunation being simply a double transit of the Sun and Moon). He showed that the low-numbered harmonics (the long waves with wide orbs) were strongly operative in the case of transits (as they are in other ways). At the time of the father's death, the transiting Sun positions revealed a strong 4th harmonic relationship to the natal Sun, and even this was enhanced in the case of lunation (the position of lunation is closely related to the transiting Sun). This is statistical evidence for the existence of transits (see the Bar Chart).

Bar Chart: Frequency of lunations prior to the father's death falling in each 15^0 of 90^0 sectors from the radical/natal Sun in the charts of 205 only sons.

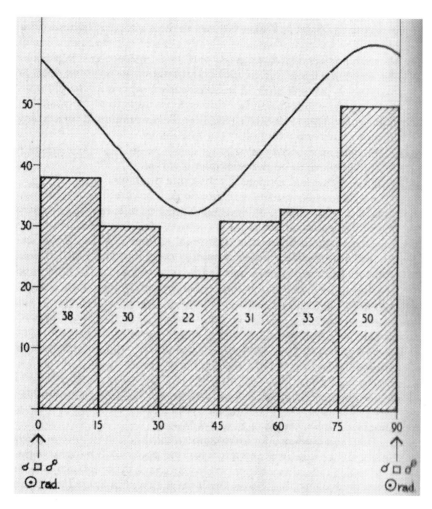

The Bar Chart shows the distribution of the lunations that preceded the father's death, relative to the natal Sun in each 90^0 sector; i.e. we are asking where the monthly conjunction of the Sun and Moon, preceding the father's death, fell in relationship to the natal Sun's position, or to the points in square or opposition to it. The 4th harmonic shows an amplitude of 38%! and is very much stronger than any other of the other shorter harmonics involved in the position of the transiting Sun.

Additionally and interestingly, Addey expressed the speculative possibility that harmonic charts in succession may apply to each year of life. Thus, the 3rd harmonic corresponds to the 3rd year and the 40th to the 40th year, and so on. This fits with an acknowledged fact about the unfolding life-process. The change from one harmonic chart to the next in the low numbers (i.e. in the early years of life) is considerable, as is our development in one year of childhood experience. Later in life, we become progressively more settled in our ways and character, so that the change from year to year (say, from the 40th to the 41st harmonic chart) is relatively small, yet still perceptible. However, we may need to identify more clearly just what we mean by 'unfoldment' in this context.

Regarding the composition of a human life (see Chapter 1) perhaps the author could be forgiven for thinking that its progress takes place under, and by means of interactions between the 1st, 3rd, 4th, 7th and 12th harmonics.

— —

CHAPTER 4

Our Present Situation Regarding Prediction

"The Beginning of Anything is Supremely Important"
C. E. O. Carter, Past President of the Astrological Association.

In our first six books, we developed an improved method for producing a complete and impartial horoscope for any person (acceptable and natural birth data permitting). We recommended a slightly modified Morinus House System (House cusps were treated as the House centres instead) as the one simple and elegant method of choice. We found that we could apply this Morinus system to the theory of 'The Pre-Natal Epoch' described by Bailey. From the Epoch (time of fertilisation) we determined the corresponding Ideal-Time-of-Birth. Impartial interpretations of Epoch and Ideal-Time-of-Birth charts were taken from books by notable astrologers and combined into an organised and understandable whole, as that person's character portrait. Character Portraits of England's royalty were compared satisfactorily with their independent biographies. In our previous book, we extended the method to include any two people in any relationship, in the process called 'Synastry', which provided a new slant on partnership.

In this book, because of its success so far, we shall try to see how the method copes with attempts at prediction from it. Bailey stated that: "Directions may be taken from the Epochal chart in exactly the same way as from the Birth chart." However, in the former case, the age of the person must be reckoned from the date of the Epoch. He was of the opinion that epochal directions supplied any deficiency in Birth chart directions when events occurred in the life that were not accounted for. Also, he said that that epochal directions could show why certain directions acted more powerfully than others.

Let us start by determining the character portrait of Queen Mary of Teck, who was King George V's royal consort. Reportedly, she was born on the 26th May, 1867 at 23:59 at Kensington Palace, London. Her Epoch occurred on the 26th September, 1866, at 16:22.

This led to an Ideal-Time-of-Birth of 23:54:36 on the 26th May, 1867. Her two natal charts of Epoch and Birth are presented in Figures 1 and 2 respectively at the end of Appendix 1, which is her character portrait. Her biography has been written by the American author, Anne Edwards, entitled: 'Matriarch: Queen Mary and the House of Windsor', 1984, ISBN 978-1-4422-3655-4.

Next, we have determined the character portrait of the 38th President of the U.S.A., Gerald R. Ford. He was born on the 14th July, 1913 at 00:49, in Omaha, Nebraska, U.S.A. His Epoch occurred on the 25th October, 1912 at 08:33. His two natal charts of Epoch and Ideal-Birth are presented in Figures 3 and 4, respectively, at the end of Appendix 2, which is his character portrait. James Cannon, an American author, has written his biography, entitled: 'Gerald R. Ford: An Honorable Life', 2013, ISBN 978-0-472-11604-1.

The most commonly used method of prediction now consists of secondary progressions of a 'Day-for-a-Year', a day being a mean solar day as a very good approximation (see R. C. Davison, "The Technique of Prediction", chapter II.) This mainly involves our 'personal' planets, namely the Sun, the Moon, Mercury, Venus and Mars, but for later-in-life events the position of the progressed Jupiter may become important. For the 'generation' planets, namely Jupiter, Saturn, Chiron, Uranus, Neptune and Pluto, we add the positions of their 'transits', i.e. their positions on a day-for-a-day basis. Transits of 'personal' planets are usually, too short to be worth considering, with the possible exception for Mercury, Venus and Mars when becoming apparently 'stationary', during times of retrograde motion. Now the passage of a transit appears to stimulate that which is already an essential part of a person's being, as given by that person's natal charts.

As with natal Astrology generally, it is the interpretations of the various progressions and transits that are significantly more imprecise than the mathematical calculations carried out to find them. Nevertheless, trends in a person's life can be seen to fit-in with what is known about that person's life, in terms of events from the person's biography. Then, by comparison, we can hope to determine that "Method of Prediction", which will become the 'method of choice'. To help here, 'Solar-Fire' computer programs (marketed by

'Astrolabe', Esoteric Technologies, Pty, Ltd.) can carry-out the required mathematical calculations for us.

Primary directions relate to the Earth's equatorial rotation; the passage of 1^0 of right ascension over the meridian (RAMC) being equated with the unfoldment of one year of life. It is rarely used, but by means of precise natal times, coupled with the use of a relevant computer program, that situation could improve.

As we have said, Secondary progressions correlate with the orbital movements of the planets; one day's movement after birth, or epoch, corresponding to one year's development of unfolding life. Transits, the secondary 'day-for-a-day' progressions are simply the everyday movements of the planets orbiting around the Sun.

Tertiary progressions, relating to one day's movement after birth, or epoch, correlate with one lunar cycle of unfolding life. We have met, and used, lunar cycles as the governing factor in our out-workings of the 'Pre-Natal Epoch' to determine the times of Epoch and their corresponding 'Ideal times of Birth'. The assumption is that these cycles continue to govern our lives even after birth. Hence measuring a life-time in terms of mean lunar cycles (like in 'Genesis'?) rather than in terms of the mean duration of the Earth's orbit around the Sun, could prove relevant, as well. In this system, the movements of the progressed planets are about 13 times larger than secondary progressions because there are that many lunar cycles of just over 27 days in one Earth year.

Regarding the Harmonic method, we follow method 3 provided by J. M. Addey in Ch. 12, p 108, in his book: 'Harmonics in Astrology', using an electronic calculator, or by computer program, 'Solar-Fire'. Addey suggested that the change in successive harmonic charts in later life was relatively small, but we found that it appeared to be much more significant than that. However, we were able to produce decimal harmonic charts, in between whole numbers, to coincide with the timing of a life-event under consideration. The planets in these charts could be placed around the corresponding natal chart in a kind of progressed manner, even though they constitute a complete harmonic chart by themselves.

— —

CHAPTER 5

Our Task – Setting-out Our Stall.

"If the method-of-choice seems surely to be the right one, but the results tend to be misleading, then probably our initial assumptions are somewhat more complicated than we had thought originally."

The two natal charts of Queen Mary (QM) and those of President Ford (PF) provide the roots (or radices) from which their lives unfold (see Figures 1-4 at the end of Chapter 4). Hence, these roots are central to any attempt at prediction, and so are individual for each person concerned. The interpretations of these natal charts has provided the material for constructing their character portraits (see Appendices 1 and 2), which, essentially, remain unchanged throughout their lives. Their comprehensive biographies give the time of any major event in their lives and indeed, our first job is to draw-up two separate lists of timed events. Then we shall try to see, how well the various methods of prediction, if any, fit with the known major events. This, of course, is 'backwards' astrology, which, later, could lead us to make actual future predictions for someone else, as 'forwards' astrology. In this way, we hope to be able to select a 'method-of-choice' for carrying out prediction. Current methods of prediction comprise, primary and secondary directions, as well as symbolic one degree-for- a-year methods. Additionally, we shall try to apply harmonic methods to see if their predictions can coincide with the timed events of each life. Finally, we hope to be able to take our 'method-of-choice' and use it to determine the future 'unfoldment' of a particular, young person's life.

Tables 1 and 2 list the major events in the lives of QM and PF respectively:-

Table 1. Life Events for Queen Mary of Teck.

Life Event	Time	Age from Birth	Age from Epoch
1) Engaged to Pr. Albert Victor	4 Nov 1891	24y 5mth	25y 1mth
Balmoral, QV, with Pr. Al. Vi.	3 Dec 1891	24y 6mth	25y 2mth
Death of Prince Albert Victor	14 Jan 1892	24y 7mth	25y 3mth
Engaged to Prince George	3 May 1893	24y 11mth	26y 7mth
Wedding to Prince George	6 Jul 1893	26y 1mth	26y 9mth
Birth of Edward VIII	23 Jun 1894	27y 1mth	27y 9mth
Birth of George VI	14 Dec 1895	28y 7mth	29y 3mth
Birth of Princess Royal	25 Apr 1897	29y 11mth	30y 8mth
Death of Mother	27 Oct 1897	30y 6mth	31y 2mth
Death of Father	Jan 1900	32y 7mth	33y 3mth
11) Birth of Prince Henry	31 Mar 1900	32y 10mth	33y 6mth
Death of QV	Jan 1901	33y 8mth	34y 4mth
Cruise to Gibraltar, etc.	16 Mar 1901	33y 10mth	34y 6mth
Return from cruise	1 Nov 1901	34y 6mth	35y 2mth
Coronation of KEVII	26 Aug 1902	35y 2mth	35y 10mth
Birth of Prince George	20 Dec 1902	35y 6mth	36y 2mth
Visit to Vienna	Apr 1904	36y 11mth	37y 6mth
Birth of Prince John	12 Jul 1905	38y 1mth	38y 9mth
Trip to India	Nv/Dc 1905	38y 6mth	39y 2mth
Trip to Spain, Ena's marriage	7 Jun 1906	39y 1mth	39y 9mth
21) Trip to Norway	Jun 1906	39y 1mth	39y 9mth
Death of KEVII	6 May 1910	42y 11mth	43y 7mth
Middle brother Frank's death	Jul 1910	43y 2mth	43y 10mth
Coronation KGV and QM	22 Jun 1911	44y 1mth	44y 9mth
Indian Durbar	Dec 1911	44y 7mth	45y 3mth
Coal strike; tour of N. of Eng.	1912	45y	45y 8mth
Visit to Germany; A. A's 90th.	Aug 1912	45y 3mth	45y 11mth
Spanish wedding	Mar 1913	45y 10mth	46y 6mth
Start of WW1	Aug 1914	47y 3mth	47y 11mth
KGV crushed by horse	28 Oct 1915	48y 5mth	49y 1mth
31) Visit to France/Spain	3 Jul 1917	50y 2mth	50y 10mth
House of Windsor est.	Jul 1917	50y 2mth	50y 10mth
End of WW1	Nov 1918	51y 6mth	52y 2mth

Death of Queen Alexandra (81)	20 Nov 1925	58y 6mth	59y 2mth
Doll's House, Lutyens	1926	59y	59y
Birth of Elizabeth, 1st grdaughter	20 Apr 1926	58y 11mth	59y 7mth
KGV ill	Nov 1928	61y 6mth	62y 2mth
To Bognor Regis	Feb 1929	61y 9mth	62y 5mth
QM and Silver Jubilee	1934-35	67 and 68y	67 and 68y
41) Death of KGV	20 Jan 1936	68y 8mth	69y 4mth
Left Buck Palace	30 Jul 1936	69y 2mth	69y 10mth
Abdication KEVIII	11 Dec 1936	69y 7mth	70y 3mth
Coronation of KGVI	12 May 1937	69y 11mth	70y 8mth
QM 70th Birthday	26 May 1937	70y 0mth	70y 8mth
D. of W. marriage	3 Jun 1937	70y 0mth	70y 8mth
WW2 in Gloucestershire	1939-45	72-78y	73-79y
Pr. George (D. of Kent) death	25 Aug 1942	75y 3mth	75y 11mth
Sandringham party – war over	Jan 1946	78y 8mth	80y 4mth
Elizabeth and Philip wedding	20 Nov 1947	80y 6mth	81y 2mth
51) KGVI arteriosclerosis start	Jan 1948	80y 7mth	81y 3mth
Charles born	14 Nov 1948	81y 6mth	82y 2mth
Bursitis return for QM	1948-9	82y 0mth	82y 8mth
Death of KGVI	6 Feb 1952	84y 8mth	85y 4mth
QM 85th birthday	26 May 1952	85y 0mth	85y 8mth
Death of QM	24 Mar 1953	85y 10mth	86y 6mth

Table 2. Life Events for President Gerald R. Ford.

Life Event	Time	Age from Birth	Age from Epoch
1) Biological parents divorced	19 Dec 1913	0y 5mth	1y 3mth
Mother and stepfather marry	1 Feb 1916	2y 6mth	3y 4mth
Joined Scouts	14 Jul 1925	12y	12y 10mth
South High School	3 Sep 1928	15y 2mth	16y 0mth
Ann Arbour, Michigan	3 Sep 1931	18y 2mth	19y 0mth
BA Economics	Jun 1935	21y 11mth	22y 9mth
Yale, to study law	Sep 1935	22y 2mth	23y 0mth
Full-time law student	Sep 1939	26y 2mth	27y 0mth
Venture into politics, NY city.	1940	27y 2mth	28y 0mth

Graduation, back to Grand Raps	1941	27y 6mth	28y 4mth
11) Pearl Harbour-joined Navy	7 Dec 1941	28y 5mth	29y 3mth
Action against Japan until	24 Dec 1944	31y 6mth	32y 4mth
Becomes 'a joiner'	Dec 1945	32y 6mth	33y 4mth
Meets Betty Warren	Sep 1947	34y 2mth	35y 0mth
Wins Republican Primary	Sep 1948	35y 2mth	36y 0mth
Marries Betty	15 Oct 1948	35y 3mth	36y 1mth
Epiphany 1, Sworn in to H o R	Jan 1949	35y 6mth	36y 4mth
2, How government spends	Nov 1950	37y 4mth	38y 2mth
3, Sent to Defence Committee	1952	39y 0mth	39y 10mth
4, travels to Korea, Japan etc.	Aug 1953	40y 1mth	40y 11mth
21) 5, Joins 'Appropriations'	1956	43y	44y
4 children born in the 1950s	1950-57	44y	45y
Helps to set-up NASA	1957	44y	45y
Ford unconcerned by election	1960	47y	48y
Stepfather dies, but elected lead	26 Jan 1962	48y 6mth	49y 4mth
President Kennedy shot	22 Nov 1963	49y 4mth	50y 2mth
Joins investig. of assassination	24 Nov 1963	49y 4mth	50y 2mth
Unhappy with Goldwater	1966	52y	53y
Ford made leader of Repubs.	4 Jan 1965	51y 6mth	52y 4mth
Death of mother (aged 75)	17 Sep 1967	54y 2mth	55y 0mth
31) National Republican Conv.	5 Aug 1968	55y 1mth	55y 11mth
Trial of 7 Watergate burglars	8 Jan 1973	59y 6mth	60y 4mth
Senate makes Ford V.P.	27 Nov 1973	60y 4mth	61y 2mth
Takes oath to become V.P.	6 Dec 1973	60y 5mth	61y 3mth
Watergate conviction	6 Aug 1974	61y 1mth	61y 11mth
Getting ready to begin	1 Jan 1975	61y 6mth	62y 4mth

Some months earlier, the Economy Policy Board warned that a recession was looming. Also, there were energy problems, as well as an imminent financial crisis in New York City. Having read the Annual Budget, it became clear that operations and costs needed trimming. As a result, a more influential Economic Policy Board was created, which, in turn led to Cabinet changes. Haig was transferred to NATO. Ford changed his method of organisation from a 'spokes of the wheel' approach to a 'pyramidal' one for staff structure, and a Code of Ethics was introduced. Rockefeller was confirmed as Vice-President (the rumour was that he was to become in charge of everything that wasn't Kissinger's!) and Edward Levi was brought in as Attorney General. Ford said that he was neither an intellectual nor an initiator, but that he liked to rise to a challenge, and to work with people of intellectual capacity, capability and independence. In the opinion of some, the final Ford Cabinet deserved to have ranked first among all the Cabinets of the 20th century, in terms of both brains and of breadth of experience. Also, National Security (Intelligence and the CIA, etc.) was reviewed. During all of the foregoing, Ford himself improved as an executive. Later, following Vietnam, he carried out the 'Hallowe'en Massacre' by reorganising and trimming the Cabinet structure. However, he was criticised for doing so.

Regarding Foreign Affairs, the Vietnam War was pre-eminent. The capture of Saigon on the 28th April, 1975, with its extraction of Americans (and Vietnamese) by helicopter, constituted Ford's 'saddest day'. However, this was countered somewhat, two weeks later, by the successful operation to rescue the crew of the 'Mayaguez'. Elsewhere, despite forging good relations with Brezhnev, no good results came from the Vladivostok meeting. Ford also met with Trudeau, Schmidt and d'Estaing resulting in a 'good' press conference.

In view of the poor economic forecasts, Ford made a 'Call for Action' in his 'State of the Union' message, but was ignored. Later, on the 17th August, 1976, he overcame Reagan to secure the Republican Nomination for President. In the subsequent election for President he lost narrowly to Carter, possibly for a badly timed comment about Poland (which later proved to be correct), the pardon he granted to Richard Nixon on the 8th September 1974, (for all the right reasons) and for demoting Vice-President Rockefeller (which made no difference). But probably he lost, because he was a far better President, than he was a Presidential candidate, i.e. he lacked showmanship quality.

Ford retired to Colorado with his family, and joined corporate boards to earn income. He pondered running for President again in 1980, but, in the event, remained loyal to his family. He died on Boxing Day, the 26th December, 2006, aged 93.

— — — — — — — — — — — — — — — — — — — —

CHAPTER 6

Backwards Astrology 1

Secondary Progressions Applied to Queen Mary's Natal Charts.

"Stronger than woe, is will – that which was good
does pass to better – and then to best."
The Light of Asia

The unusual, natal charts of Queen Mary (QM) (see Figures 1 and 2) are useful for us, to start with, because both Morin Points lie in the 1st Pisces decanate. This means that both progressed charts will proceed along similar lines. Additionally, all four life events that we have chosen for her, take place in London. This should simplify the overall assessment of her individual future. Then we can use the experience gained with her charts for more usual charts, such as those of President Ford (PF).

Beginning then with QM's charts, we take in turn, four major events from Table 1, Chapter 5, p 28, namely her marriage (1893), her coronation (1911), the December, 1936 abdication crisis concerning her eldest son, King Edward VIII, and her death in March, 1953. We shall also begin by using the currently most favoured method of prediction involving secondary progressions, coupled with transits.

Combined charts (Figures 7 and 8, see pp 48 and 49) show her Epoch and Birth charts in the centre circles surrounded by the adjacent concentric ring containing her 'personal' progressed planets for 22th June, 1911, together with the outer concentric ring containing her transiting 'generation' planets for that day. Interpretations (none of which are mine) of her charts are taken mostly from Alan Leo's book, "The Progressed Horoscope", but when the planet Pluto is involved, then they are taken from R. C. Davison's book, "The Technique of Prediction". The step-by-step process of producing her four individual futures is given later, but here we present the four individual futures as 'backwards, combined and organised interpretations'. Thus:-

The backwards, combined and organised interpretations for the time of QM's marriage on the 6th July, 1893 at 15:00, in London, comprise:-

[X 2 There would have been changes either in residency, occupation, acquaintances, habits and/or travelling. She would have had to be careful not to make mistakes, and would have had to prepare for the changes of condition that were forthcoming. She should have guarded against becoming too critical, or too fault-finding.] She should have remained careful of her own interests, and even have been suspicious of others. She would have become more ambitious for her relatively limited ideas of that time, and would have been likely to have had responsibility placed upon her, or to have taken-on a task, in which tact and diplomacy would have been required. As a result, there would have been control by older persons, or with those who had some authority over her. Possibly, spiritual experiences would have been met also during this time, but she should have avoided any disclosures that may have led to trouble and unpleasantness for her, with her property, with her father, with her elders, as well as with her further, future education.

[X 2 Mary would have wanted to lead, and to have been recognised in her new position. Mental energy, coupled with considerable enthusiasm, would have been evident. She would have become more interested in, and keen about, life, wishing to gain all the useful knowledge that she could. A prosperous and pleasant time would have been anticipated.] She would have experienced a joyful period and a time of complete satisfaction, in which financial matters would have prospered strongly. Her prospects would have looked brighter and happier than they had done for some time. This situation would have cultivated her feelings and higher emotions splendidly at her time of marriage. Much reciprocal generosity and consideration between the two marriage partners would have ensued. All these benefits would have greatly improved all of her conditions and affairs. She should have taken full advantage while this time lasted, i.e. 'have made hay, while the sun shines'.

Furthermore, an investigation of the deeper side of religion, philosophy, science and/or the psychic, would have been possible at this happy time.

— —

The backwards, combined and organised interpretations for QM's Coronation on the 22ⁿᵈ June, 1911 at 15:00, in London, (see Figures 7 and 8) comprise:-

There was the promise of the beginning of a more fortunate period providing light and life. Her prospects would have looked brighter and happier than they would have done for some time. [X 2 Here was a period of opportunities that would have come at no other time, and the secret would have lain in her expansive and fullness of expression. This would have been a favourable time for her mind, for foreign affairs and for benefits from abroad.] She would have had a somewhat philosophical and religious frame of mind, and this would have marked the beginning of her loftier views. But also, new ideas may have arisen and would have directed her thought, once again, towards science, philosophy, invention and the psychic. In addition, there was another good influence operating, but not in material affairs. This would have brought opportunities for consolidation and for making conditions more permanent. There would have been greater responsibility along with a rise in status, whereby her honour and her reputation would have benefitted. It would have been up to her, and her methods, to gain the most favourable results from this particular influence.

If she had taken advantage of all these opportunities, then she could have joined head and heart, and so have accomplished her mission in life, namely, the conversion of thought into wisdom. Feelings would have been brought prominently into her life, and would have awakened the deeper side of her sympathies. This would have been the influence of summer that follows spring, and would have denoted a period when some of her further ambitions would have been realised; when by virtue of her mind and her power, she would have risen to a higher and better state of being.

QM would have experienced a new and congenial society, thereby making new friends. Moreover, changes in habits, or in some new undertaking, might have begun. In fact, this would have been a good time for coming before the public, i.e. in dealing with the many, and for making new journeys. There would have been business with lawyers and merchants, as well as with educationalists. Thus many advantages leading to much progress, would have been taken. It would have been a good time for travel, and even for undertaking long journeys/sea voyages. However, caution would also have been required during this period regarding travel, as well as with correspondence. She may have been encouraged to make changes in her attitude to charitable affairs, but she tended to show a lack of feeling for charity, which could have led to difficulties.

Some happening, or illness, would have been likely to cause sorrow and meditation, but which could have led to an expansion of consciousness. However, this would have been followed by a practical, dogmatic and perhaps severe mental state, despite brightness and activity. Care would have been necessary to avoid going to extremes, coupled with hasty speech, and with a tendency to become sarcastic. Some ruthlessness might well have been shown (so do unto others as you would be done by!) but there was also the possibility for self-denial, and even for asceticism, during this period. Additionally, there could have been domestic trouble, followed by a desire for rest.

— — — — — — — — — — — — — — — — — — —

Figure 7: Secondary Progressions and Transits for QM's Coronation at 15:00, on 22nd June, 1911, from Epoch.

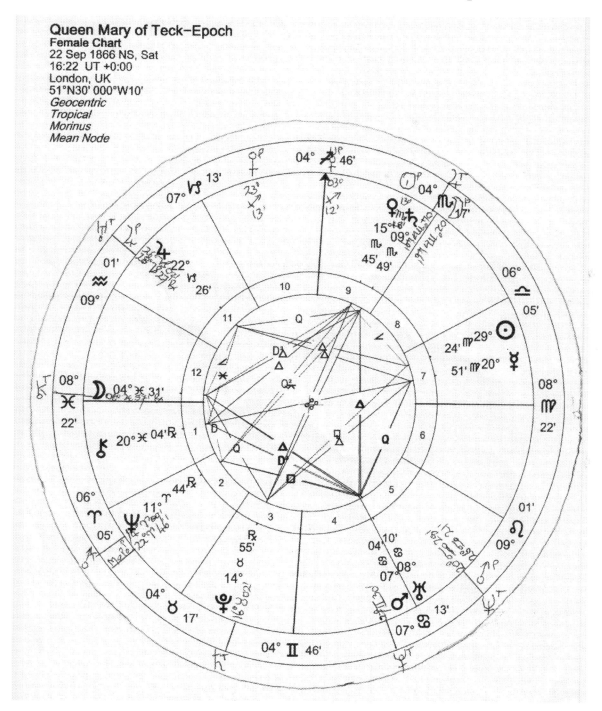

Figure 8: Secondary Progressions and Transits for QM's
          Coronation at 15:00, on 22nd June, 1911, from Birth.

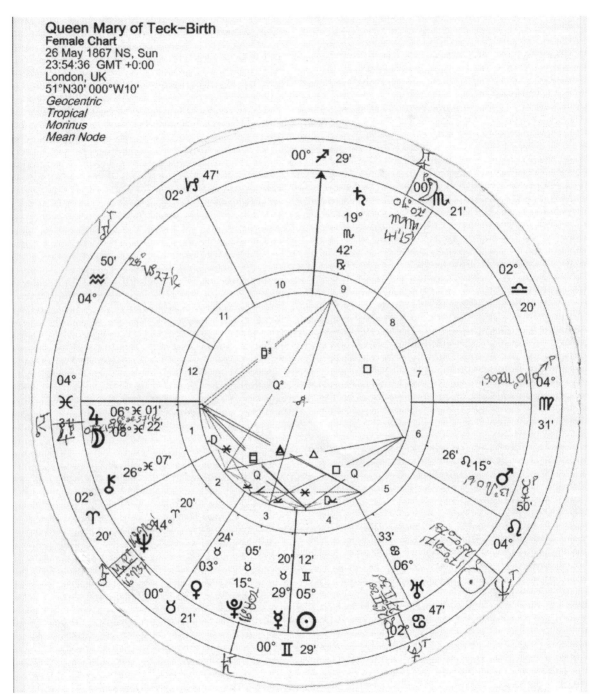

The backwards, combined and organised interpretations for QM during the Abdication crisis of 11th December, 1936 at 12:00 in London comprise:

[X 2 QM's mind would now have become more discriminating and critical, resulting in her becoming intuitively and imaginatively, perceptive. She would have had the ability to analyse all things critically – including herself!] Also, this was a time to improve her mind generally, e.g. making for study and for rapid learning.

[X 2 QM would have had experiences in connection with sickness, nursing and health matters. Responding to these changes would have benefitted her in many ways, such as becoming more solid and practical.] A more firm and reliable attitude would have been induced. Additionally, she may have received helpful advice from someone older than herself.

Concurrently, there would have been an argumentative, independent and vital time, during which she may have suffered from feverish complaints. She may have moved house, and have made mistakes of judgement, resulting in a turbulent frame of mind.

Other influences having been favourable, which perhaps they weren't, this period could have proved to be one of religious and spiritual blessing. However, deaths may have affected her. For possibly a month, strange, uncommon and absurd events may have been met. Also, her dreams may have been remarkable and unpleasant. She should have taken great care not to become involved with scams, frauds and undesirable persons.

QM's charity would have been very steady, sincere and honest, despite depressing circumstances current in her mind. There may have been attempts to change her attitude to charitable affairs, which may have proved to be troublesome and harassing. These could have brought responsibility, but a careful and patient frame of mind would have contributed caution, reserve and tactfulness. She should have acted discreetly through all attempts at fraudulent deception, and in all her philanthropic affairs.

[Perhaps interestingly, and generally, transits at London, at midday, on the 11th December, 1936, formed a mutable grand-cross at the Morinus 'angles'. This consisted of Saturn at the Morin Point opposing Neptune, and the Sun at the centre of the 10th House opposing Chiron.

This configuration implies an adjustment to conditions, and an attempt to by-pass them, but rarely without nervous stress.]

— —

The backwards, combined and organised interpretations for the death of QM at 10:35 a.m. on the 24th March, 1953, in London, consist of:-

[X 2 Despite some pleasant and beneficial changes, her mind and nervous system would have been affected unfavourably, leading her to brood over her conditions, and desiring in vain, to alter in some way, the environment in which she was placed. Her thinking would have become deeper, being drawn towards objects and externals, rather than towards intangibles. Additionally, a further influence may have served only to exacerbate her frustration. However, there was also a temporary, favourable influence, which would have brought a more steady and thoughtful mind, tending to alleviate mental troubles, making her peaceful and well-disposed. Her thoughts could have become uplifted through clairvoyance, sometimes facilitated by listening to her preferred music. This would have been a good time for independent thought and freedom from personal bias. To help here, there would have been an increased ability to reach conclusions by means of flashes of inspiration, rather than through more orthodox, reasoning methods. Whereas she would have aspired after mental attainments, thereby inclining her to travel, and to make her wish to contact close relatives, this could have caused frustration and despair. However, friends could have brought her pleasure.

At this generally unfortunate period, her health would have suffered through a lack of vitality, and through depletion. A favourable influence upon her person was now weakening. She may have suffered from blood disorders, and ill-health through excess bile, or surfeit. Yet her feelings and emotions could have been favourably excited, with benefit from elders, causing her to respond with affection, sympathy and friendship. She could have determined courageously, not to have given way to despondent, remorseful feelings.

There would have been gain through philanthropy, and this would have been a good time for terminating any important matters.

— —

CHAPTER 7

Tertiary Progressions applied to Queen Mary's Natal Charts

"The Moon is nothing but a circumambulatory aphrodisiac."
Christopher Fry, 'A Sleep of Prisoners'

Instead of using the progression method of one-day-for-a-year, i.e. one day of the Earth's rotation about its axis, is taken to be equivalent to the duration of the Earth's orbit around the Sun, here, similarly, we use one-day-for-a-lunar-cycle of about 27.3 days, being the duration of the Moon's orbit around the Earth. Previously, we have met lunar cycles as the major factor in our determination of Ideal Birth times using the Pre-Natal Epoch. After birth, it is just possible that lunar cycles continue to function as controlling factors in the composition and course of a human life.

We have also suggested that the gravitational pull of the Moon in its orbit around the Earth was strong enough to catalyse the formation of optically-active, life-chemicals (such as *laevo*-rotatory amino-acids, leading on to optically active peptides and then to chiral, capable-of-forming-coils, proteins) needed for the production of the following appearance of Life-on-Earth. We know that self-sustaining life only started at one, particular period (not relatively long after 4.5 billion years ago) so that when time passed, and the Moon receded from its close proximity with the Earth, then its gravitational force became insufficient to kick-start the formation of life-on-Earth, ever again. In addition, we have suggested that the early, strong, gravitational pull of the Moon constitutes a Prime cause for producing life-on-Earth, as evidenced by the optical activity of life-chemical compounds.

Accordingly, and once again, consider Figure 5, consisting of three concentric circles with a natal chart occupying the centre one, and with the transits occupying the outer rim. Only the inner rim undergoes change and now will contain the tertiary progressed planets and Morin Point, for QM's wedding day, in this case; instead of those of the secondary progressions. Now let us examine the:-

Backwards, combined and organised interpretations of her natal charts, for the time and place of QM's marriage using tertiary progressions.

QM would have been over-anxious and inclined to worry. Her gloomy, brooding and melancholic side would have been brought out, making her liable to become depressed, or despondent. There would have been the possibility of chills, troubles with the elderly, and with her honour, reputation and family affairs. She should have guarded against poisons, or from suffering harm through drugs. There would have been problems with her health, much opposition and many obstacles would have been placed along her path. There would have been disappointments, losses by death in the family circle, as well as sorrows and trials of many kinds in domestic affairs. As a result, she could not have acted too wisely, for her mind would have tended to despair; she would ever have looked on the dark side of things, and she would have met persons whose influence would not have been beneficial. Also, there would have been antagonism between her moral character and selfishness, as well as between generosity and over-carefulness. All these tendencies would have needed combatting by a firm will, and she would have required all her care and forethought, to have kept her head above water. Her attitude should have been based on the idea that, "whatever is, is best". This would have been a very critical, yet memorable period.

On the other hand, matters regarding friendship could have become prominent. She may have developed a love of animals, or dumb life, causing an awakening of her deeper sympathies. She would have become more hospitable, and her sympathy for others much broader. She should have tried to make the most of opportunities that would have come her way. This may have been a good time to improve conditions financially, socially, domestically and with friends. Yet a hampering, or restrictive, influence of some kind, there was sure to have been.

Additionally, all matters of financial concern would have come to the fore. Those who could have taken advantage of this, could nearly always have found ways to increase their income. Recently, and generally, a critical period had been passing, during which she should have avoided litigation, extravagance or lavish generosity, for waste was taking place, either in her physical system, or in her surroundings. She would have been inclined to over-enthusiasm, or to an excess of feeling, for both social affairs and religious matters. Also, there was a liability to lose money. She should have watched her expenditure, and have checked any waste occurring in her affairs. Also, she should have avoided excess in her diet, and have exercised temperance. She should neither have lent nor borrowed money, and have become surety for none.

This would have been a good time for those having inspirational and imaginative qualities coupled with a flair for history. As a result of a more clear-sighted approach to the World, QM may have developed an ability to perceive the true motives of others, and have become able to play on their susceptibilities. She would have become very refined, and have taken a deeper interest in intellectual pursuits. She would have developed literary tastes, and have engaged in correspondence. She would have found refined friends among kindred, or relatives, who would have helped her. Her mind would have become more active, so that she would have been living in the mental side of her nature. She would have tended to express herself more readily. She may well have been able to make herself better understood than usual. Independent thought was favoured, with freedom from personal bias. This would have been a good time to study and learn, to plan and arrange, and her brain would have responded. Also, there may have been a desire for self-purification, leading on to self-discipline and to self-denial.

There would have been a contrast between her desire for expansion and increase, with her internal, spiritual and moral nature. She may have had difficulty in achieving a blend between her ideals and her personal desires. Neurotic complaints could have developed. Social, or religious, disputes were likely to have caused her some anxiety. However, her mind may have been influenced by the realisation of a rare exaltation, of a more or less ecstatic character, due to poetic, or to musical, inspiration. Certain dreams may have been remembered!

QM would have found it easier to get on with others by means of more refined and sensitive feelings; these would have tended to be precipitate, and so would have brought about a premature consummation, or sudden termination, of attachments. For now, the unexpected always happened. But her affections and emotions would have been stimulated to their highest pitch, thereby affecting her impressionability. Certainly, she would not have been apathetic, or callous, at this time.

A general rise in QM's life would have been met with social activity and possibly gain. It could have led to a very prosperous and successful time. She would have seen clearly the best course to adopt for general improvement and success. She would either have travelled, or have made important, beneficial changes.

At this time, QM had reached an epoch in her life. The opportunities that lay before her would have surpassed any of those she had met in her past, or would have met in her future. Hence, she should, in every way, have made the most of this favourable time. She would have obtained advancement, social success and would have had the satisfaction of seeing her ambitions gratified. She would have formed lasting and permanent attachments, and would have become linked with others to mutual advantage; all things would have gone right for her. There would have been permanent bonds formed, both helpful and profitable. She would have felt generously and kindly disposed to all with whom she came into contact. She would have met helpful people and have expanded her sympathies as well as her religious sentiments.

QM's mind would have become intuitive, showing sound judgement, and would have been full of common-sense. Her consciousness would have now expanded, and she would have gained by investment and travel. Her nervous system would have improved, dealings with inferiors would have become profitable, and she could now have engaged agents to manage her affairs honestly and discreetly. She would have had success with writings concerned with papers and legal transactions.

At the same time, QM would have become more steady, thoughtful, careful and prudent. She would have sought to act with great discretion, and would have ordered her affairs wisely and systematically. Her dealings would have gone well and she would have thought about the virtues of purity, chastity and temperance.

Her mind would have been improved, being made more sober and earnest. It would have been good for contracts and engagements.

Later on, her own wisdom would have been stimulated, as well as her powers of judgement, coupled with her ability to organise her resources. As the result of integrity and hard work, she would have gained advancement and increased business sense.

The question of charity would also have been brought to the fore. Her stimulated mental side would have made this a good time for learning about it. Her sound judgement, and enhanced maturity would have made for a more optimistic outlook regarding her charitable affairs.

— — — — — — — — — — — — — — — — — — — —

Tertiary Progressions applied to QM's Natal Charts for her Coronation on 22nd June, 1911 at 15:00, in London.

Backwards, combined and organised interpretations for the time and place of QM's coronation using tertiary progressions.

Not long before her coronation, QM may have found that her mind had become obscured by vague and indeterminate fears, longings and aspirations, but which may have led to a pre-destined expansion of consciousness. For example, she may have been stimulated to study those things that lie beneath the surface, such as an opportunity for travel.

QM had now reached a second epoch in her life, because the opportunities that now lay before her would have surpassed any of those that she had had for a long time, or would have had again in her near future. Hence, she should have made the most of this favourable time. She could now have invested, have formed lasting and permanent attachments, have become linked to others to mutual advantage, and all things would have gone right for her. This material and spiritual, thrice-in-a-lifetime influence would have enabled her to gain a deeper insight into religious matters, to become more philosophical, and so more thoughtful and wise in her actions. She would have become more uplifted, improved and prosperous – just as she chose.

QM would have become more aware of the latent possibilities of her nature. She would now have gained a more stable frame of mind, which would have caused her to become more social, independent and free. She would have had a more artistic condition, hitherto more or less latent. She would have made some lasting, faithful and helpful friendships. She would have become more refined and more inclined towards metaphysical and subjective types of study. Her humanitarian side would have been awakened, and she would have understood character and human nature with ease. She would have become pure-minded, have had potent desires, and have refined her expression, during this time.

QM would have become more determined and very firm in her decisions. Through fixity of purpose, she would have brought her ambitions to a successful conclusion, but there would have been a dangerous side to this influence. She would have gained some knowledge of her own inherent power, and this would have aroused any pride, or dignity, also latent in her nature. She may well have experienced feelings of jealousy, and so could have been inclined to sarcastic and caustic utterances when vexed, or offended. Hence, the gentler side of her nature would have been over-laid by this apparently coarser vibration. Possibly, this would have brought troubles and sorrows. However occult, mystical and psychic attractions would have given her the ability to get in touch with the deeper part of her nature. In turn, this would have brought out all her sympathies, truly hopeful tendencies and done much to stir-up her deeper emotions. She would have become more than usually secretive, and during the time ahead, would have experienced more than she had done, for much time in her past. However, provided that she had made no enemies previously, then she need not have feared any troubles, because in part, this was the time for the fruit of past actions to work out its own destiny, both through any suffering, coupled with the wisdom gained thereby.

Two keywords for a concurrent influence are 'impulse' and 'expression'. This can lead to love-at-first-sight, or to some very hasty decisions that affect the feelings and emotions. Provided that QM could have quelled her desire for sensation, and refrained from rash conduct, then this current influence could have made her liberal and free. As a result, she would have met success through her quick response to mirth, cheerfulness and readiness to take part in any pleasure, or gaiety that may have come her way. This is the joining of the "Soul with the Senses", bringing a fuller and more sensuous expression of either, than otherwise had been the case. Had the soul been stronger, then love would have prevailed, but if the senses, then the soul would have become their captive. The situation seemed to have been that her passions would have overcome her feelings, but nevertheless on an harmonious and peaceful level. However, because her energies and passions had been stimulated, care would have been needed not to arouse enmity by over-assertiveness. But if soul and senses had been matched, then a liberal time would have lain before her.

A further, concurrent influence would have had the keywords, 'sudden' and 'precipitate', thereby bringing a premature consummation, or an immediate termination, of any attachment formed. The magnetic conditions of others may have moved her to actions that would have had a lasting effect upon her life. It may be said that, "the unexpected always happens", because nothing would have transpired as she would have expected. She would have been more than usually idealistic, imaginative and susceptible to the influence of others, and would have sought to act as independently and originally as her nature would have permitted. Certainly, she would not have been apathetic, or callous, at this time.

Moreover, another influence could have produced an involved state of affairs in every phase of activity. Deep frustration may have led to some rash act. But opportunities for a fresh phase of experience and achievement, through dynamic leadership, was possible. In fact, re-orientation of her life may have resulted.

A joyful period would now have been upon her, during which QM would have experienced much satisfaction, because all would have gone as 'merrily as a marriage bell'. This, like all good influences, could have been used for both material and spiritual ends. There may even have been the spiritual possibility for ecstasy, illumination and mystical vision! Indeed, emotional activity and artistic sensibilities would perhaps have led to some inner transformation. This coming of bright joy in her life may have made it one of her most happy and successful times.

However, there were also some stressful influences in operation at the same time. Thus, her mind could have become too acute and over-active, so that she should have guarded against indiscretion in speech, rash action, or in too much assertiveness. Additionally, wrong-headedness, wrong people, involvement in religious disputes, mistakes of judgement, monetary losses, frauds, scams and extravagant outlay on personal ostentation, could have led to set-backs. This would have been a poor time for disputes in general, with a liability to suffer from the disfavour of others, including inferiors. She needed to look to her honour, trust and integrity, and have done nothing likely to produce scandal, or to injure her responsibilities and reputation. Strange episodes, remarkable and unpleasant dreams, uncommon fancies, as well as the absurd, may have occurred. As an advanced person, this period could well have made a marked impression. She had to have cultivated a cautious and common-sense approach to her problems during this period, for inflammation, together with mental activity, could have produced a turbulent frame of mind.

More pleasantly, there were also influences to bring about various changes that would have been fortunate and beneficial in their effect. There may have been changes in occupation, in habit, in understanding, or in pursuit, and in friends. She could have become more interested in philosophy, religion and possibly, the occult. Voyages are sometimes indicated, which would have applied to QM. These influences could also have proved fortunate for coming before the public, or for dealing with the many, or for a journey. They would have been good for health, domestic and household matters, even though these influences tend to be weak.

Her mentality would have been stimulated towards reading, education, literary work, speaking, travelling and would have included her relations with siblings, and with the young, generally. Her increased mental effort would have made her freer, more liberal and braver. It would have helped her to travel by supplying the 'go' that she may have required. She should have let this work out through her ambitions, rather than through her mind and senses, thereby promoting good health and enterprise. Any transformation within her would have been supported. Also, her tendency would have been to enlarge the scope of her personal expression in financial matters, perhaps at the temporary expense of artistic, helpful and cheerful affairs. Her personal, charitable affairs would have been more favoured, while bearing in mind her radical, stressed, attitude towards these.

— —

Tertiary Progressions Applied to QM's Natal Charts for the Abdication Crisis of 11th December, 1936 at 12:00, in London.

Having met with a steady and enduring time, during which stability of character and persevering tendencies improved her general conditions, QM would have become more grave and seriously disposed, as well as being industrious and painstaking. During this time, a strange influence was passing away. Neither benefit, nor harmony would have acted well. QM would have found this influence trying, and in turn, affairs between her and those to whom she would have been attached, or in any way bound by sympathy and affection, would not have gone smoothly. However, a liability to deception, weird experiences, remarkable dreams and fanciful actions would have soon been over.

All of this would have tended to lessen, or disorganise, QM's vitality. There would have been delay, or loss, in connection with her occupation and affairs. Leading persons in the social World may not have been well-disposed towards her at this time. She should have tried to avoid conflict with them, or with those connected with the law. Her public position, or reputation, may have suffered, and there may have been loss of credit, the disfavour of superiors, and sorrow through friends. Someone, to whom she was attached, could have gone abroad, or would have had important engagements, necessitating a separation at this time. Yet there was a mixture of sorrow and pleasure under this influence, so that with care, it would not have affected her too seriously. In fact, this period was not likely to have been that eventful, and so, no matter how important any other influence may have seemed, it would have had far less potency and power to affect her life, for good or ill.

Soon QM would have entered a softer critical, and less selfish side, bringing more intuition and receptivity into her life. She would have found herself becoming more obstinate, or self-willed, or more stubborn and firm, but she may have turned this into determination and strength of purpose. True obedience, which gives all the sympathetic qualities, coupled with an eager mentality, i.e. love and intellect combined, resulted in an obedient service of the highest kind. At her most successful, she would have worked for the sake of work, without the motive of self at the back of the effort, which is a very high ideal. She would have come into contact with someone older than herself, whose advice may have proved helpful.

QM would now have had a much firmer and more stable frame of mind, which would have caused her to become more sociable, independent and free; for her social and artistic condition, hitherto more or less latent, would have been awakened. She would have been able to study and to comprehend character and human nature with ease. Her mentality would have been inclined towards the more metaphysical and subjective type of study. It would have been a good time for travel, for making changes and for dealing with relatives and kindred. Writing and correspondence would have been favoured, resulting in rapid progress. Even charitable affairs could have benefitted. She would have become pure-minded, have had potent desires and have made much progress in purity of thought, and in refinement of expression, during the time of this influence. If she could have abstracted some inner virtue too, then she would have found it leading to the study of higher thought, as well as of occult, or mystical, subjects.

QM would have felt more than usually sympathetic and tolerant. Also, she may have felt a tendency to nervous disorders with some inclination to become easily impressed, whimsical and sentimental. She had needed to be careful not to fall too much under the influence of others. There may have been troubles through women and difficulties with affections and attachments. At the same time, a beneficial influence, as well as an harmonious mental vibration, would not have worked well. Affairs between QM and those to whom she may have been attached, would not have gone smoothly. Yet she would have discharged her duties more faithfully, and have become more conscious of her actions, while this influence lasted.

QM would now have found improved financial conditions, so that this would have been a good time to engage in investment and speculation, both with prudence, as well as to have sought pleasures generally. Those who are able to take advantage here, could nearly always have found means to increase their income by judicious investment, or through engaging their minds in financial affairs for their own benefit. Also, this influence would have been good for those who have the inspiration and imagination for historical writing. However, another influence could have caused some financial losses, losses through travel and through dealings with religious persons. After a draining period upon her purse, if she could have exercised thrift, and have diligently placed herself in a permanent position, then this influence could have worked beneficially.

QMs health could have become disturbed due to a loss of vitality. There may have been some difficulty, regarding her generative system. Additionally, poor health may have restricted her activities through colds, chills, rheumatism and accidents of the falling, crashing kind.

— — — — — — — — — — — — — — — — — — —

Tertiary Progressions Applied to QM's Natal Charts for her Death on the 24th March, 1953 at 10:35, in London – Backwards, Combined and Organised.

QM would have begun to show a firmer and more determined tendency in her nature. A favourable influence would have brought a sobering and steadying affect into her life. She would have become much more practical in her aims, and simultaneously, more dogmatic in her opinions. She may even have become irritable and abrupt, leading her to repent later. Also, she would have become impressionable and easily influenced. She may have become more liable to make mistakes, more erratic and more fanciful, as well as becoming prone to act more through personal bias rather than from any well-defined motives. However, her other tendency would have been to display a greater spirit of obedience. She would have tried to become silent, persistent and calm, in recognition of the power of her internal will, which could have commanded, because she would have had the latent power to obey. Thus, "whosoever will be chief among you, let him/her be your servant."

QM's mind would have acquired a philosophical, independent and penetrative, as well as religious, overlay, which would have marked the advent of loftier views. There would have been success in affairs of the higher mind. Probably, this would have awakened her desire to investigate the deeper problems and inner mysteries relating to consciousness, and to the future. There would have been the promise of a more fortunate period commencing. She would have become more thoughtful and serious, with a strong inclination to carry-out her duty without any hesitation, so that if she had been ready for the new vibration, then she would have become persevering, thrifty, careful, prudent and thoroughly trustworthy. There would have been an extra impetus towards religious thought.

However, there was a more perilous influence, too. QM's mind would have become obscured by vague and indeterminate fears, longings and aspirations, so much so that her moral sense may have become quite perverted. She may have achieved an unenviable notoriety through some evil deed. Understanding and control would have been needed here. Otherwise fraud and deception would have been likely to cause the sorrow and meditation that may have led to the expansion of consciousness, which this influence had been destined to lead to.

In addition, there was an influence fortunate for family affairs, as well as for making new friends, acquaintances, for mixing in society, for pleasure seeking, holiday making, travel, love affairs and for general, good fortune. She would have got on well with elderly persons, and would have made new friends and acquaintances among them, also. This was an influence during which QM's passions may have become excited, but not powerfully. Simply by taking care, she would have avoided any troubles caused by her acting rashly.

But friendships may have suffered, and there could have been disappointment and sorrows through her affections. Deliberation would have been necessary regarding the emotional side of her nature. She needed to pay attention to developing her sympathies, bearing in mind to follow the motto:- "Do unto others, as she would be done by." It may have been a good time to make herself active with regard to feelings, so that her affections may have found a safe outlet. She would have been allowed to give vent to her emotions along lines of least resistance, which would have been offered during this time.

Moreover, there was a fortunate influence that would have brought about changes of various kinds that were pleasant, or beneficial, in their effect. There may have been a change in occupation, or in habits; some new undertaking, or pursuit, may have begun. It would have been good for general affairs, such as domestic and household matters. Also, it would have been fortunate for coming before the public, and for dealing with the many, or for travel. There may have been an opportunity for going abroad, or for taking some very long journey. Furthermore, it would have been a good time for undertaking new responsibilities, or for beginning new enterprises. It would have brought good fortune through superiors, the great and those in authority, as well as through friends ruled by the Sun. Some amount of public recognition, honour, or fame, would have followed. She would either have gained promotion, or otherwise have become important in some way. Her credit would have improved and she would have gained some standing in the sphere in which she moved, or have done something that would have advanced her interests, making sure and steady progress towards a better state of affairs. Now, she should have done all that she could to obtain a permanent post, or to have arranged her affairs onto a substantial foundation. Moreover, this would have been a good time for those who have the inspiration and imagination required for historical writing.

All matters connected with finance would have been brought to the fore. This was a good time for those who are able to take advantage of this influence, and nearly always would have found means to increase their incomes, either through judicious investment, or by engaging their minds in general financial affairs for their own benefit. QM would have become more interested in money matters, which may have led to increased prosperity. It would have been a good time to seek pleasures generally, with success through travel. She may have gained by investing in the mineral sources of the Earth. Also, she may have gained through legacies. QM may have become very generous and liberal, and unless she had been careful to avoid excess of any kind, she may have taken her extravagance to extremes. Conversely, there may have been financial reverses in matters connected with the sea, or air, transport, and with oil, or gases.

In addition, troubles with charitable affairs could possibly have caused anxiety and worry. QM may have become too rash concerning charitable activities. She had to have been careful in her dealings with charity workers to avoid fraud, and to have guarded against being imposed upon by others. There was an influence tending to prevent her charitable affairs from coming to fruition. But QM's charitable affairs could have become more pleasure-loving and peaceful. There was an influence that could signify, temporarily, an important change in charitable attitude. However, this charitable quickening would have been the forerunner of greater activities to come in the future, rather than being the immediate indicator of events. As such, it would have depended for outward effect very much on further, future, beneficial influences rather than on those that were current.

Following two fortunate influences for QM's health and vitality, her bodily energy would have supported her, allowing her to cope with normal occupation. However, the rash expenditure of her physical resources may have lowered her resistance to disease. Her liver was likely to have become her most vulnerable organ. Also, her health may have been affected by nervous debility, or eyestrain. In addition, there may have been danger of accidents with gas, or noxious fumes. Furthermore, her health may have been affected by troubles with the bony structure, such as bursitis, with bruises and skin diseases due to the accumulation of poisons in her system over a long period. QM had some liability to suffer from taking poisons, or from being harmfully affected by the side-effects of drugs, or medicines, if care had not been taken. Such diseases resulting, would often have been difficult to diagnose, and even more difficult to cure.

— — — — — — — — — — — — — — — — — — —

CHAPTER 8

Primary Directions and Harmonic Charts

The method of the 'progressed horoscope' that includes 'Secondary Progressions', is based mainly on the orbital revolution of the Earth (around the Sun), and on the apparent orbital movements of the Sun, Moon and planets (around the Earth). Mostly, it uses the day-for-a-year method for calculations. The method of 'Primary Directions' is based mainly on the Earth's daily axial rotation, wherein the heavenly bodies are made to rise, culminate and set. Mostly, it uses the degree-for-a-year method for its calculations, which is considerably more onerous and time consuming than that used to obtain 'Secondary' and 'Tertiary' progressions. However, the use of a computer program (Solar-Fire) obviates these disadvantages. Also, with 'Primary Directions', it is necessary that the birth time should be known very precisely, or should have been carefully rectified, because a difference of Right Ascension of the Meridian (or its equivalent of four minutes of Sidereal [star] time) will introduce an error that will amount to, on average, one year in the determination of the times that directions will apply. But regarding careful rectification, the 'Ideal Birth Time' derived from the use of the 'Theory of the Pre-Natal Epoch' could well be substituted usefully here.

In addition, 'Primary Directions' are all formed within a few hours after birth; each four minutes of star time, (or, for what amounts to be the same thing, the passage of each degree of Right Ascension across the meridian) measures to one year of life. At this rate, we can see that all the 'Directions' in the life of a person that is 100 years old, are formed completely within 100 X 4 = 400 minutes, or 6 hours and 40 minutes. This seems extremely fatalistic! Why 'Directions' that are formed within 7 hours after birth should not produce their effect in the life-history until a great many years afterwards, is a problem that needs to be relegated to the esoteric department of Astrology. On the other hand, our present understanding of the workings of time, is poor, at best.

'Secondary' and 'Tertiary' progressions take longer to form at the rate of one day for each year, or for each lunar cycle, of life. The fact that they are not completed until long after the 'Primary Directions' is the real reason why they are labelled 'Secondary' or 'Tertiary', in point of time, but they still resemble 'Primary Directions' because they are completed in the horoscope long before they produce their effect in the outer World. Thus, a 'Secondary' progression that operates at the age of 100, will have formed 100 days, or roughly 14 weeks, after birth (or 3 years and 8 months after birth for 'Tertiary' progressions).

Whereas 'Secondary' and 'Tertiary' progressions depend upon the movements of the Sun, Moon and planets after birth (or epoch) as shown in an ephemeris, 'Primary Directions' are all formed by the rotation of the Earth on its axis, and bear no relation, essentially, to the movements of the other heavenly bodies in the Zodiac that remain almost unaffected. The movements of the Sun, Moon and planets through the Zodiac after birth/epoch belong only to the 'Secondary' and 'Tertiary' systems.

Probably, we derive our physical form, as well as our character, from our DNA. Analogously, we derive our physical form and our character from the interpretations of our natal charts. These are two expressions of the same thing. This leads us to suggest that our natal charts can stand as a more tractable form of our DNA giving us the interpretations for intangible characteristics. Because we all seem to be members of the Solar system (somehow through our links with DNA) even though, naturally, we are all Earthlings first, we shall concentrate our efforts at prediction mainly on the 'Secondary' and 'Tertiary' systems rather than on the relatively more insular 'Primary Directions' system.

Despite the foregoing, rather negative assessment of 'Primary Directions', van Dam, in Holland, has developed a computer program recently for obtaining van Dam 'Primary Directions' (related to C. C. Massey in Alan Leo, 'The Progressed Horoscope', p 331?) that has produced good results. Also, Deborah Houlding has published (2009) an easy method for understanding 'Primary Directions' and the Federation of American Astrologers has produced a translation of 'Morin's Directions' (1994) from the French into English. A Solar-Fire computer program has allowed us to produce a striking van

Dam chart for Queen Mary of Teck's death, from her Epoch chart. Nevertheless, we shall continue with the 'Progressions' systems for now, for the reasons given above. But first, let us take a look at:-

Harmonic Charts

Instead of using a <u>day</u>-for-a-year (or for a lunar cycle) or a <u>degree</u>-for-a-year (or lunar cycle), we can use an <u>harmonic number</u>-for-a-year (or lunar cycle). Thus, the beginning point for the first year of life, i.e. either from the time of birth, or epoch, is chosen as the time to start the 1st harmonic. At his/her 1st birthday we have the start of the 2nd year of life, from which we produce the 2nd harmonic chart, and so on, up to the age at the death of the person. For example, in the case of the 5th harmonic chart, we envisage the whole circle (360^0) as divided into 5 smaller zodiacs, each of 72^0, and each comprising the 12 signs, each one of 6^0 in extent. The next job is to determine how we calculate, from the radical chart, the positions of the Sun, Moon and planets in the 5th harmonic chart. To do this we use an electronic calculator. It consists of multiplying the radical longitude of each heavenly body (i.e. from 0^0 Aries) by 5 (the number of the harmonic required) and then subtracting from the answer the nearest smaller multiple of the 360^0 of a full circle. The value of the remainder gives the new harmonic position in the 5th harmonic chart.

Let us suppose that the radical Moon's longitude position is 23^0 33' Scorpio. In terms of a full circle, this equals 7 X 30 = 210^0 + 23^0 33' = 233^0 33'. We multiply this by 5 to give 1167^0 45'. Now we subtract 3 X 360^0 = 1080^0 to give a remainder of 87^0 45' that equates to 27^0 45' Gemini and this is the position of the 5th harmonic Moon. In order to carry out these calculations electronically, we need to express the radical positions in degrees and decimals of a degree. Hence, 23^0 33' Scorpio would be entered as 233.55^0, which is multiplied by 5, 3 X 360^0 is subtracted, and then the decimal part of the answer is converted back to minutes of a degree by multiplying it by 60. When all the radical positions – including the Ascendant – have been recalculated in terms of the 5th harmonic, we plot them all into one chart. Notice, however, that in order to do this satisfactorily, we have to use the sizes are not fully equal. But if required, we can convert the 5th harmonic, Equal House Ascendant back to an equivalent Morin Point easily.

Now there is the possibility, according to Addey (see 'Harmonics in Astrology' p 165) that the harmonic charts in succession may apply to each year of life, as we have indicated, so that the 40th harmonic corresponds to the 40th year of life, etc. Once again, a computer program in Solar-Fire, does all the work for us, and can in fact do it for all relevant harmonics - let's say up to 100 – as well as including three decimal places, such as the 35.627th harmonic, for example.

Our approach now is as follows: Firstly, we take the Epoch and the Birth chart and from them produce a person's character portrait. This is his/her fundamental character throughout life. Then we take an important event in the person's life – let's say marriage – and calculate his/her age as accurately as possible in years and decimals of a year from his/her epoch and birth times (these will differ on average by about 9 months) to the time and date of the event. We use the Solar-Fire program to generate the respective harmonic charts for the two different ages at the event time. We then derive a character portrait overlay from the interpretations of these two charts, and then try to decide how relevant this character overlay was (we are still conducting 'backwards' astrology) for the time of the event. The interpretations of House positions in harmonic charts tend to be excluded because House centres are no longer actual, but serve only to symbolise the significance of the House centres.

Consider now the wedding of Queen Mary of Teck at 15:00 on the 6th July, 1893, in London. Appendix 1 has provided us with her character portrait from the interpretations of her Epoch and Birth charts (see Figures 1 and 2). We require the accurate harmonic facts concerning her age in years and in decimals of a year. We find that her age from Epoch was 26.711 years and her age from Birth was 26.112 years.

Character Overlay for QM's Wedding from Harmonic, Epoch and Birth Charts

Character

General

QM would have shown her good nature, sincerity and helpfulness, with mental power as well as imagination. She had a tendency to squander gains, to be extravagant, and to trust to luck too easily. She could have been moody, or quarrelsome, and a tendency to rash action should have been restrained strongly. Life, on or by the sea, would have been liked.

Mentality

QM was both subjective and objective, with optimism in her nature. Also, there was refinement and popularity, along with artistic, or musical ability. She showed an interest in travel, and in acquiring foreign languages.

QM's mind worked in a "far-flung" manner. Restless because she was far-seeking, yet she could have become satisfied by knowledge. QM's personality would have been out-of-the-ordinary; clever, original, seeking new and interesting ways, such as in science and aviation, even if letting go of the old. QM's speech was quick and decisive. On the other hand, her mind could have become acute, excitable and acrimonious. Her awakened ambition, combined with a very strong personality, as well as coupled with very quick and accurate perception, resulted in great power of comparison. Additionally, her mind threw off worries easily, and began thought anew. Although she showed strength and freedom-loving expansiveness, there would have been some limitation to herself, as well as some difficulty of expression. There was a need for her to guard against deception. Her ideals were keen and strong, and although her assertiveness was softened, there was also a tendency to use her imagination to give strength to her ideals, but in the event, prejudicially. Thus, her vivid imagination tended to be gullible and confused, so that her mind was not well-directed. Touchiness induced escapism. Her mind would have schemed in an involved way, yet action would have been from intuition, rather than from reason. Ideas that seemed inspirational would have been better, if well-scrutinised.

Communication took place in affairs relating to more profound studies, as well as in those to do with home, domesticity and any business to do with collecting. Mental occupations would have been conducted at home.

Lifestyle

QM's life had a characteristic and important direction of interest. There would have been a particular and uncompromising direction to her life-effort. She may have shown some interest in a cause, but with much less concern about end-results, and with no desire to conserve either herself, or her resources. She developed a balancing of life-emphases at contrasting points in her experience. It would have been a persistent move to a balance, which was apt to show a characteristic rhythm, and could have been described over-literally as a teeter-totter. At all times, there was a tendency to act under a consideration of opposing views, or to a sensitiveness to contrasting and antagonistic possibilities. She existed mainly in a World of conflicts, of definite polarisations.

Effort would have been made to obtain her ideals in unusual ways, but tension could have snapped, causing tragedy. QM's self-will, independence, and desire to make breaks and start anew, would have found relevant and assertive expression. She showed an intention to surmount her difficulties. QM herself, became able to assert herself, in stressful situations, while staying calm and composed, which could have given her an advantage over adversaries. Unfortunately, she tended to allow her critical faculty, and constant fuss over details, to interfere with the harmony of her life. Yet, on balance, she would have been able to be happy. Relief may have been found by letting her energies free themselves in happier activities, as indicated in her natal charts. She showed a tendency to develop harmony, rhythm and beauty, as well as artistic expression, psychic sensitivity and "hunches". She would have become acquisitive and so likely to accumulate money, or property, as well as being desirous of wealth. Partly as a result, she would have been inclined to upsets and to forced new phases.

Relationships

Others

Possibly, QM would have been liable to suffer, and to cause harm to others, in the attempt to get to the top, yet she continued to meet helpful people. When others spoke, she listened carefully, and picked-up many ideas. She was inclined to expect position through affection, but she would have been too strict with younger people. Wilfulness and insistence on being different, produced tactlessness and bluntness, which offended others. Her relationships with women were not easy.

Friends

Her friends would have been helpful.

Family

She would not have got-on very well with her parents, and would have become separated from them. She would have inherited little from them. Probably, she had learned a lot from her father, but he might have expected a lot in return. Relations with her mother would not have been easy. Affairs of siblings could have proved to give cause for attention, and she would have been too practical with loved ones. Thus, there was a lack of harmony at home, but force, combined with control, could have proved useful for the bearing of personal hardships.

Lover

Her early conditioning and emotional apprehension about handling people who became too familiar, would have passed eventually. There was an uneasy expression of affections, so that her life tended to become solitary. But she could have developed an ability to express her internal feelings. Yet the tendency remained that her affections and partnerships were subject to disclosures, upheavals and new starts, with trouble and unpleasantness. Any partnership brought responsibility. Her sense of lack intensified her shyness and had tended to prevent an easy response to what would have brought happiness. Her unusualness was apt to be fascinating and compulsive, but not that pleasant. Partnerships were unconventional, may have proved to be difficult, and were apt to be broken because of insistence on freedom. Thus, partings were likely through unhappy causes. Hence, there was sorrow and loss through her affections.

QM may have wanted to marry just to compensate for the early family ties that she had missed, which may have made it difficult for her to be comfortable on her own. She needed someone with a strong identity, who would have given her the attention she needed. She needed a partner who understood her, and who would have supported her, when her self-confidence had sagged. In fact, she would have enjoyed being married, and having a family. Her partner may have been more helpful to her than she had expected, and so she should have paid attention to any suggestions that he had offered, because, probably, they would have proved to be beneficial. He could have become her best source of inspiration, and both he and she would have been rewarded by living up to each other's expectations.

Career

Intro:

Her destiny lay mainly in the hands of others, but also in her own hands. There was a tendency to a lucky journey through life, even to the meeting of good opportunities. There was benefit from hidden sources, with a fortune from speculation and investment, leading to prosperity.

Early

There would have been a cleavage in her life relating to her parents. The resulting disharmony in her nature could have urged her to accomplishment. Lessons of duty and self-control would have been learnt, but she would have felt inadequate in home matters. As she was 'always on the go', overdoing needed using-up in her career. She was vigorous, worked to an end, and showed a keen desire to plan and succeed. 'Work and energy were put into a day's work!' There was keenness to get to the top in material ways. It was likely that she would have enjoyed success early in her career. There would have been an overlay of courage, enterprise and a notable capacity for administration. She had to have become increasingly independent, so that she could have asserted herself in her career. Good intentions may not have been good enough. She knew that to do her best work, she must have become fully informed. She would even have gone without some of her favourite comforts, and would have spent time, energy and work to gain her goals successfully. This would have involved sacrifice, but she knew that this would have assured her future security, and her independence, from want. As a result, she became more practical and ambitious, which gave her aptitude for business pursuits. Also, she became more suited for a public, or commercial, career, rather than for one in a family. Obstacles would have come into her life, but her ambitions would have stayed keen, and there would have been a love of fame, a desire to lead along with an ambition to govern. However, her force tended to be frittered away in constant change of direction. Nevertheless, she would have been apt to adopt her allegiances to lines along which she could have made her efforts count for the most. Additionally, there may have been some deception involved, or some liability to gullibility. Her highest priority should have been her willingness to take-on the challenges of competition. There was no easy way for her to gain public recognition for her accomplishments, except through self-discipline and her determination to succeed. This would have inspired her self-image and assured her of growth in her position. Even her competitors could have served her purpose, provided that she had learnt how they had succeeded. Nothing annoyed her more than the competitor who had tried to intimidate her into conceding defeat, without a confrontation.

Vocation

QM had a special capacity, or a gift, or an ability for some specific kind of activity. At her best, she could have been a real inspirer, or instructor, of others; but at her worst, an agitator, or malcontent. The fruits of her imagination would have been used in works of art, of literature, in psychism, or in intuition in everyday and professional life. There was keenness to work at educational and literary pursuits.

Working with young people would have seemed ideal for her; and directing people in their creative development and creative expression, were areas in which she could have succeeded. There were enthusiasms for the arts, dancing and idealism. Work was done to achieve well with these, even though they may have been visionary and unattainable. Eccentricity was shown in taking care of anyone, or anything. All forms of mediumship and psychic ability would have been developable. She would have become mentally aware of, and would have had some inclination to become interested in, charity.

Middle

QM would have become capable of unique achievement through a development of unsuspected relations in life, but was apt to waste her energies through her somewhat improper alignment with various situations. Energy and limitation did not combine well, unless force and initiative could have been canalised, and caution enlivened. If so, then these would have been helpful for all arduous, rough, or pioneering conditions.

QM tended to be compulsive and magnetic, so that leadership was either obeyed, or violently broken. Sensitive tendencies may have been brought to better fulfilment, due to the compulsion of stress, but at the same time, her escapism may have prevailed, leading perhaps to deceit and/or gullibility.

Late

QM could have tended to become disappointed with her public career, as well as with life, in general.

Appearance and Health

Health

QM would have had good health, but her nervous system could have been vulnerable. There would have been a tenseness that was hard to relax, and which tended to cause nerve storms. However, sleep would have been good, dreams frequent and anaesthetics taken well.

— — — — — — — — — — — — — — — — — — — —

Character Overlay for QM's Coronation from harmonic Epoch and Birth Charts combined.

Character

<u>General:</u> QM's self-expression would have been shown energetically. She would have felt vigorous, courageous, initiatory, bold, mentally hard-working and quick. She would have had an intention to surmount her difficulties. She appeared cheerful, contented, independent, interested and dramatic. Happiness was shown in domestic conditions. She would have had a good, balanced outlook, coupled with a love of beauty and with interests in the arts. Music, dancing, poetry and painting would have become necessities of life. Although her inclination would have been towards beauty and ease, it would have been too irresponsible and lazy. Similarly, there would have been a tendency to squander gains, be extravagant and to trust to luck too easily. Her restless personality may have been tempered by an easy-going and comfort-loving disposition. But her moods and ways could have been changeful in an acceptable way, since new phases in life were liked. There would have been a characteristic love of travel and change from youth to old-age. Psychic sensitivity would have been absent rarely, and could have been developed like any other gift. "Clouds of glory" were more to have been expected than any delusion. Her ideas and 'hunches' should have been acted upon. Life, on or by the sea, would have been liked.

QM would have loved to be 'spoilt', have had plenty of amusement and have indulged in social life. However, this would not have been that successful. There may have developed a receptive, self-distrustful disposition showing reserve, diffidence and coldness, but a positive and quietly affectionate nature could have been called-out easily. Although much may have been achieved, her tendency would have been to overstrain through overdoing. Her constructiveness, in a narrow, one-track way, tended to become rigid discipline and dreary planning.

More negatively, QM could have become self-seeking, assertive, aggressive, magnetic, pugnacious and bad-tempered, at times. There would have been a moody, or quarrelsome nature with a tendency to become explosive. In addition, her magnetism could have been stimulated easily towards sensation. Such behaviour was likely to end conditions and force new beginnings, with unhappy results. She would have insisted on her right to assert herself, when she got the impulse. She didn't feel that she had to explain her actions to anyone, and she didn't. Her behaviour, at such times, appeared to be based on a belief in the survival of the fittest.

<u>Mentality:</u> QM was both objective and subjective. Her mind would have been powerful, courageous and enterprising. She had a good, common-sense mentality, combined with nervous force. Well to the fore would have been the virtues of prudence, steadiness, charm-of-speech, pleasantness of manner along with the generally beneficial result of an harmoniously working nervous system. All these would have improved her mind and mental outlook. Her talent for dialogue was one of her best assets. Her mind may well have worked fluently, quickly and with versatility, but possibly also excessively, over-rationally and under-emotionally. Much could have been done in a quiet way. This steady, useful disposition, coupled with her esteem, worked well but rarely would have become fortunate in a Worldly sense.

QM's sensitive psyche was opened through her unconscious and much would have been given out through the reception of ideas and influences. She may have seemed magnetic, with tendencies towards scientific thought, originality and rebelliousness. Although this sensitivity may have been brought to good result through compulsion and difficulty, she would have needed to guard against escapism. Her ideas and intuitions were strong, but may have been carried out perversely, cantankerously and with strain. Fortunately, her mind could have thrown-off worries easily, and have begun new thought with relief; but occasionally, over-violently and explosively, with increased tension. Mental loneliness could have resulted through fear and apprehension. Lack of poise could have led to brusque speech and writing.

Additionally, QM's mind could have become over-widened, so that it lost grasp, producing carelessness, woolly-thinking and indiscretion. Her vivid imagination, which could have become gullible and confused, then may have lacked good direction. Her resulting touchiness would have induced escapism, her mind would have schemed in an involved way, and action would have come through intuition, rather than from reason. Hence magnetic leadership, coupled with unusual ability, could have led to explosive temper, wilful impatience and strain. However, strong control of these negative traits, would have been possible also.

Lifestyle: QM focused strongly on achieving a comfortable and abundant lifestyle, enriched by a rewarding career and good friends. In order to fit into the social environment she aspired to, she may have had to overspend in order to acquire the right social image. Being accepted was very important to her. However, she fitted quite naturally into the mainstream of society, and because of her easy-going manner and flair for communication, generally she would have qualified to join the groups of people that she wanted to.

Because of her natural curiosity, QM accumulated considerable knowledge about many subjects. While her ability to retain information was notable, sometimes she had difficulty disseminating between fact and fiction. This was because she allowed her feelings to interfere with her logic, which resulted in an emotional bias even in important matters. In her eagerness to communicate what she knew, she tended to take liberties with the facts, especially when she wanted to impress people. At times, perhaps unfortunately, she believed truly that events actually had occurred as she had related them.

A person with QM's planets distributed at every angle (of her harmonic Birth chart may well have 'got on her horse and ridden-off in every direction'. However, at her best, she would have shown a capacity for a general, universal interest and a gift for ordering what, to a lesser ability, might have seemed to be utter confusion. This is the fundamental relationship of all things, by means of which the 'Universe' comprises a consistent whole (shades of 'Simply Now'?) More particularly, her harmonic birth chart shows her greatest possible resort to particular, immediate and practical self-responsibility. Neptune provides the focus (being Earth, cardinal and angular, as well as part of the accompanying cardinal T-square) for the over-emphasised sensitiveness of this special type. As a result, she should have assumed that her relationships were not all what they seemed. Her ideal may have been based on romantic fantasy, making disappointment likely, when she had seen her situation in the harsh light of reality. However, and again, she did have a great deal of self-control.

Additionally, QM would have felt set-off from a definite part of the World, i.e. she felt excluded, in some subtle fashion, from a complete segment of experience. Not only did she have something, but that this something was placed into a relationship within a larger consideration. Her occupied segment, containing her planets, reveals her activity and organisation, and this would have become her response to the challenge to her existence, presented by the unoccupied segment, according to its needs and emptiness. There would have been a marked sense of what she contained, contrasted with what she could not have held. This would have taken the form of an advocacy of some cause, the furtherance of a mission, or of an introspective concern over the purpose of experience.

QM would always have had something to give to her fellows, whether literally or psychologically, or whether constructively or vindictively, because her orientation to her World arose from division, i.e. from frustration and uncertainty. Her Mars – Venus conjunction at harmonic Epoch shows where and how, as a person, she would have sought to carry out her mission (or gain her everyday justification for existence). She would have become more self-expanding (or more self-seeking) and more practically interested in what things mean, and in what they are. She may have preferred to initiate experience, rather than to consummate various phases of life. Furthermore, she may well have become more idealistic.

Relationships

<u>Others:</u> QM showed an overlay of friendliness and cheerfulness. She knew how to make people feel comfortable, which endeared her to them. Especially, she was skilled in dealing with people in her personal and professional affairs. There was a love of pleasure and of social life that helped to bring popularity. Possibly, a tendency to become too easy-going could have led to difficulties, unless firmly controlled. Usually, she had the last word in a conversation, but then she had initiated it also. She showed people easily that she was well-informed, and she stimulated them to enter freely into conversation with her. She had a deep need to relate to others professionally and socially, and she utilised her creative ideas better through the people she was involved with. However, lingering ties to her family may have made her inwardly apprehensive that she would not have been accepted.

On occasion, she may have had difficulty with people, who resented her lack of inhibition. In addition, her relations with women may not have been easy. She could have been hurtful and selfish with others. Also, she took enormous chances that she wouldn't have encountered someone who would have resisted her more strongly than she would have bargained for. But unless she could have accommodated other people's needs, she may never have felt that she'd made any contribution to society.

<u>Friends:</u> QM would have been on good terms with most of her friends, and she was happy to do favours for them, knowing that they would have reciprocated. She took advantage of opportunities provided by her friends, and she didn't forget favours that she had received in the past. Nevertheless, she had to have paid more attention to her friends' suggestions for achieving her goals. Although at the time, she may have considered herself obliged to help her friends when they expected favours, she also knew that when she had realised her goals, she would have had the financial security to indulge only those who had merited her attention.

QM wanted to be first among her friends in everything that she did. But the uncertainty of the future should have warned her to use her energy more prudently. However, her tactlessness sometimes antagonised her friends. Thus, there could well have been breaks with them.

Family: QM's parents may not have understood her need to have her own identity, and may not have given her opportunities to grow and mature in a direction that would have been exclusively her own. Her parents may have deeply infiltrated her consciousness, forcing her to qualify her opinions and views, so that these would have met with her parents' approval. Her parents may not have intended to subvert her own thinking, but the result was the same as if they had planned it that way. She would have become conditioned to feel guilty, if she hadn't concurred with her mother's views, resulting in a diminished ability to express herself. Also, she may have had to struggle to establish her own authority, after having coped with her father as an authority figure. She would have followed closely along parental lines, both in character and occupation, but also, a great change may have occurred, and an entirely new environment and occupation would have been taken-up. It would have been absolutely necessary for her to get involved with persons outside her family, and getting an education may have been the ideal way to serve that purpose. She should have got out on her own, as soon as possible.

On the other hand, her parents may have allowed her to express herself in her own way, so that she would have assumed that everyone would have allowed her that privilege. In this case, probably, she would have continued to enjoy a favourable relationship with her parents. Also, the affairs of her brothers would have mattered.

QM quarrelled easily with loved ones. There was a lack of peace in her home, and an uneasy expression of affection would have resulted in a lack of harmony there. Breaks in personal relationships could have occurred.

QM had many plans for her children, and she hoped that they would have taken advantage of the training she'd provided to achieve on their own. Although having a family curtailed her freedom to come and go as she pleased, she could have accepted this restraint because she knew that they would have become as independent and self-sufficient, as she would have allowed them to be.

<u>Lover:</u> QM had fairly good judgement in handling relationships. There was a love of display, and of attraction towards men. She had an ability to love and to enjoy sexual life, and all things of beauty, strongly and robustly, but less delicately. She made subtle demands on her romantic partners, and she didn't take rejection gracefully. Partnerships were very important to her, but if her partners hadn't co-operated, then she easily forgot that they existed. Her affection was most difficult to express, so that life tended to be solitary. Any partnership brought responsibility, sorrow and loss, through her affections. Also, pre-occupation with her career may have made a dent in her romantic life, and have been disturbing to her lover. Thus, her affections and partnerships tended to be subject to disclosures, upheavals and new starts, accompanied by trouble and unpleasantness. As a result, her nature would have become harder (and possibly more selfish) with pride and vindictiveness, especially connected with her feelings. She had a strong desire nature, and wouldn't have accepted 'no' for an answer. A cutting harshness could have entered into relationships of affection. Feelings would have been strong, which both caused and received hurt. Sexual relations were likely to have been intense, but not without quarrels. Hence, partnerships wouldn't have been easy. Despite control, there could have been troubles in partnerships, marriage and business.

And so, a sense of lack intensified her shyness, and could have prevented an easy response to what could have brought happiness. When she had been attracted to someone, she had to have asked a trusted friend for an unbiased opinion. Alternatively, she may have found someone, who was desperate for her to serve his own needs. In that case, she could well have found a parasite, who would have clung to her, until she had felt strangled. As a result, she had to have been extremely cautious about building any relationship.

A disappointing childhood may have conditioned her to escape into marriage, which was hardly the best reason for such a demanding relationship. She might have chosen someone, who was as insecure as herself, out of sentimental pity. But having a permanent partner would have provided her with emotional comfort, so that she could have directed her efforts to her career. However, she had to have been sure of her lover's affection, before making a commitment. She mustn't have assumed that it was love, just because she desired it. She looked for a partner who was on the way up, or who showed promise. She enhanced her partner's social position, and he would have shared her dreams for the future. Her partner must have supported her in her drive for success; he must have been as eager as she was, for it. She would have derived much satisfaction from indulging her mate. For his part, he had to have accepted her as she was, because it was nearly impossible for her to change.

Sometimes, her happiness would have been secret.

Career

QM's destiny would lie in her own hands, in the hands of others and would have depended on circumstances. She would have had a changeful career, but new phases in life were liked. There would have been opportunities, good luck and success. Also, there would have been spiritual progress, and a useful life.

Early: Alienating circumstances in her home would have forced QM to assert herself and feel confident, so that she would have been able to succeed on her own. But they may also have allowed her to express herself, and to have become involved in the World around her – an ideal situation for continuing development and success. The public would have accepted her, which would have simplified her taking her place before the World. Her love of people and her high ideals gave her a responsibility to use her creativity for the benefit of others. But this creativity could have failed her, unless she had realised how important it was for her to develop her talents. She needed to get as much education as she could afford, to help to ensure that others couldn't have exploited her for their own benefit. She hadn't to do anything without a plan, and she mustn't have deviated from it. She had to have defined her goals and to have made sure that she adhered to them rigidly, in order to achieve them.

QM attracted people who were hypnotised by her compelling desire to rise above her early circumstances. Also, she would have become a prime target for people who would have taken advantage of her talents. She had to have distrusted everyone, until she knew that they could have been trusted. Serving others was one thing, but being exploited was another.

Although QM may have preferred to bide her time, until she had felt sure that she could have succeeded in her endeavours, she knew that someday she would have made an important impact on society. She would have been willing to cultivate her talents quietly, until she had arrived at the right moment for using them. But she had to have guarded against family obligations from interfering with her development of creativity, thereby delaying her independence. Also, she found it difficult to sacrifice any of her desires, yet some sacrifice would have been necessary as an investment, in order to achieve the long-range goals that she had set for herself. However, when given the opportunity, she proved that she could have promoted her ideas to achieve the goals she'd established. She refused to get involved in any situation that didn't use her creativity to the maximum. Additionally, she had to have been a friend to others, and to have reaped their loyalty in return. Moreover, she had to have chosen a career that allowed her self-determination and some freedom, otherwise she would have felt ineffectual. A career, in which she worked with large numbers of people, whose future depended on her, would have been so much the better.

Vocation: QM's intuition was active and backed by critical inspiration. She was able, a good worker in a variety of directions, and so possessed of fairly good, all-round abilities. Her mental nature was well-developed, such that intuition and intellect blended very well. A good education would have made her suitable for any of the higher pursuits: literary, legal, or medical, for instance, or she could have been well-adapted for business. Whatever career she chose, she must have been certain to have had enough room to grow and develop to the best of her potential. There would have been so much that she could have accomplished, if she had had the determination to pursue it. She would have found satisfaction in politics, journalism, government service, news service, broadcasting, design, or in architecture.

QM felt a strong spiritual dedication to serving the needs of her fellows, and she demanded the opportunity to prove herself. Because she liked people, and had a talent for dealing with them, she might have sought a career in communications. She would have been excellent in any career that brought her into close contact with the public, such as education, counselling, selling, or social services. She should have directed her attention to those who needed her understanding and compassion. She could have worked most effectively with children who had learning disabilities, and who required sympathetic understanding. She could have shown them how to become self-sufficient.

QM indulged in much self-analysis, which made her reasonably familiar with people's motivations. Communication took place in affairs connected with reading, writing and educational matters.

Possibly, good results would have accrued from enthusiasm for the arts and idealism. Work would have done to achieve these, even if visionary and unobtainable.

There could have been success in magical and psychic affairs.

Middle: QM was sensitive, curious and ingenious at promoting herself, which tended to make her popular. Gaining public attention turned her on, but unless she had had a genuine contribution to make, then the public would have easily been turned-off by her actions. Generally, she knew what people wanted, and she offered herself as the person most qualified to provide it. She wasn't afraid to promote herself, and she was convincing enough to win people's confidence. She didn't form secret alliances with so-called friends, who may have been using her to satisfy their own objectives. Being well-informed at all times, should have prevented this. The tendency was that her imagination worked overtime, developing ways to exploit her creativity. But she was also inclined to discuss her ideas too freely with others, which encouraged plagiarism. Probably, her greatest opportunities would have come through appreciating and learning from other people's opinions. She tried to live each day as fully as possible, for she knew that her future security and independence depended on it. Security became more important to her than previously, but often she failed to plan ahead for security because she was so fascinated with the present. She realised that her future lay in her own hands and that she wouldn't have felt fulfilled until she had seen tangible evidence for her success. She realised too, that she must plan ahead, so that she would have been prepared when opportunity came along. She had to try to be specific about what she hoped to achieve, and wasn't to be misled by well-meaning friends. Constructiveness could have forced to a patient working-out of what had been started, but not with ease. Results must have been battled for. The narrowness engendered produced selfishness and egocentricity. Hardness was endured and sternness given. The practical became over-valued, with a tendency to meet hardships. Moreover, subtle and difficult-to-detect problems were possible. Thus, her imaginative and intuitional aims would have required all of her strength and control to actualise them.

QM could have accomplished almost anything, if she had been willing to sacrifice some immediate pleasures. After she had fulfilled the demands of her career, she should have made plans to get involved in fulfilling social needs.

Charity: QM's charity was facilitated by activity, expansiveness and could have become forceful and incisive. The general tendency was that common-sense and creativity supported her charitable activities, as well as in helping to direct them.

Late: QM knew how to put her ideas to work for her later years, when she would have wanted to be free from obligation. Yet she needed to plan more efficiently, so that she would not have become burned out from exhaustion. Her gift for creative imagination only needed application in order to help her to realise her goals and provide her with the financial security for her later years. However, QM would have gained the resources earlier, which she will have needed for her security, later.

Appearance and Health

<u>Appearance:</u> QM was a good-looking woman with an attractive personality.

<u>Health:</u> QM had good health and strength was given to her nervous system as evidenced by good eyesight, hearing and sense of touch. However, any weakness in her nervous system would have caused worry that, in turn, could have led to intestinal trouble. Overdoing would have impaired her vitality, making her liable to minor accidents, such as burns, scalds, falling and accidents to limbs. Perhaps these would have been brought on by irritation, bad temper and nervous tension. Yet she would have remained a good sleeper. Any gullibility, deception, lack of direction, woolly thinking and indiscretion may have found its cause in a lack of correct working between her liver with her nervous system.

— —

The Present State of the Exercise to determine a Method-of-Choice for obtaining Our Individual Futures.

1. <u>Secondary Progressions</u> consisting of progressed 'personal' planets together with transiting 'generation' planets – the most popular method. The duration of the progressions seems to be rather long, whereas the duration of the transits appears to be rather short, but the combined method overall, seems satisfactory. There appears to be reasonably good agreement between what happened at all four important life stages with the descriptions obtained from interpretations of the relevant charts. Now we require to apply this method to President Ford's charts, and to extend any suitable conclusions reached to making predictions for a young person's life.
2. <u>Tertiary Progressions plus some Transits.</u> The durations of tertiary progressions is significantly shorter than those for secondary ones but we can extend their use up to, and including Saturn. The duration of transits remains unchanged, but we

could choose to use fewer of them, other factors being equal. The descriptions of interpretations do not seem to fit quite as well for QM's life events, particularly for her time of death, as do those of secondary ones. For comparison purposes with secondary, we should apply this method to President Ford's charts and to extend any useful conclusions from it, to determine the predictions for a young person's life.

3. <u>Primary Directions.</u> For reasons already presented (see Chapter 6) we shall not continue with this method of prediction, either for President Ford, or for a the events young person's life.

4. <u>The Harmonic Method,</u> first suggested by J. M. Addey, and including the harmonic position of the Epoch and Birth chart Morin Points, almost produces complete charts, from which we can make interpretations for producing general descriptions. In the case of each of QM's four life events, these descriptions don't appear to describe these events, but simply seem to add to the original descriptions obtained from the radical/funda-mental Epoch and Birth charts. Possibly, this might have been expected from a relationship between an harmonic chart and its corresponding fundamental/radical one. As a result, we shall not continue to use this method for any further determinations of individual futures.

However, one factor common to all the prediction charts is that there are significantly more aspects between the Sun and Mercury, the Sun and Venus and between Mercury and Venus, than are possible in the radical charts themselves, due to geometrical and physical limitations. In the radical charts, Mercury is never further than 28^0 from the Sun; Venus is never further than 48^0 from the Sun and Mercury is never more than 76^0 from Venus.

— — — — — — — — — — — — — — — — — — — —

CHAPTER 9

President Gerald R. Ford

Backwards Astrology 2

Now let us consider the predictions from the secondary and tertiary progressions of PF's natal charts coupled with transits (which are the same for both charts for a specific event time). Figures 3 and 4 have shown that his Epoch and Birth charts are rather different form QM's charts, because the Morin Points are different. This is a more usual situation, but the interpretations obtained will be somewhat longer. His secondary progressed charts for his time when he stepped-up to become Vice-President on the 13th October, 1973, to be precise, are presented at the end of the section on 'Becoming Vice-President and President'. But before that we shall examine the predictions for his epiphany and marriage at the end of 1948 provided by the secondary method. After that, we shall compare the predictions of the two methods surrounding his death on Boxing Day, 2006. This is not to be macabre, but allows to compare most favourably, the secondary interpretations with the tertiary ones to see which method provides us with the more relevant results. We should then have determined the 'method of choice' for carrying out prediction.

— — — — — — — — — — — — — — — — — — — —

Epiphany and Marriage of Gerald Ford, October, 1948 – January, 1949 from his Epoch and Birth Charts, by their Secondary Progressions and Transits.

Backwards Astrology 2

Character

General: Physically, this will have been a more positive time, but not necessarily good for affairs in general. Vigour, vitality, cheerfulness, hope and opportunity were available to take advantage of as personal abilities, but anxiety would have been caused through personal pleasures.

Mentality: Gerald's mind would have become more active, i.e. enquiring and diligent. There would have been more correspondence, an accession to thoughtfulness and he would have acquired an enhanced sense of refinement. His mind would have been awakened, new, inventive thought of some kind would have occurred and made manifest an attraction towards science and/or philosophy. Progress would have been made in study, research, speech making and in transport activities. In a short time, Gerald would have become more critical, more inclined towards higher thought, more optimistic and more aware of the importance of detail. He would have improved his expression as well as his ability to take advantage of opportunity. The more his mind became stimulated, the more alert and operative he would have become. Useful work, done at this time, would have been good, not only for this time, but also for the future. In addition, his prudence in speech, conduct and in large responsibility, would have been enhanced. His strict scrutiny of moral conduct would have become developed, and there would have been an increased desire for independence and freedom. Moreover, he would have wanted to study those things that lay beneath the surface, but he might have fallen prey to wrong ideas brought about through mass suggestion, which had connected with his inner compulsion. Originality and inventive conclusions were reached through flashes of inspiration, plus a contribution of Gerald's own to the current methods of others, coupled with an ability to act suddenly, at an opportunistic moment.

Thus, he would have shown group leadership of a dynamic kind, but needed to guard against acting in too eccentric, or self-willed fashion. However, and concurrently, his inventive and original ability, would have been starting to decline.

Also, this may have been a good time to study telepathy, and to receive new thought.

Lifestyle: An earlier influence, perhaps two years before, would have made Gerald's mind overly sharp, causing him to over-reach himself, leading to quarrels and opposition. Thus, care would have been needed now. An unfortunate influence would have followed, ending in uncertainty, worry, indecision, unpopularity and disfavour. This would not have been good for general affairs. A third influence could have signalled the start of a 'highly critical period'.

Acquisitiveness would have been brought into Gerald's desire nature, which would have caused him to acquire wealth. Now he could have become more persistent, plodding and working-on to his desired goals quietly and cautiously, yet with determination. He would have found increased intuition regarding both material and spiritual things, but also a very practical and common-sense attitude towards everything. This would have been a good time for the thrifty and painstaking side of his nature, but otherwise indifferent. His sterner virtues would have become studied and practical. Gerald's greatest success would have come from pure-living, and from a lack of obstinacy for standing in his own light. Firmness and determination would have been obtained.

Probably, Gerald would have received some responsibility, and certainly his sense of justice and moral tendencies would have been brought out and accentuated. His position would have become elevated, giving him advantages for progress and stimulation, thereby making him try to improve his surroundings. This would have been a good time for asking for favours, and simultaneously for raising himself to a higher level of efficiency and service. All matters of business would have come to the fore and his work would have become prominent in his life. Additionally, there would have been domestic arrangements, the material side of his life would have been affected, and more general activity would have entered his life. As a result, Gerald would have been brought into an entirely new set of conditions, either, or both, physical and mental. Now he would have aspired more eagerly after mental attainments, seeking further knowledge.

Relationships

Others: Gerald may have felt more sympathetic and tolerant than usual. He should have acted calmly and peacefully, so that he could feel good influences. Social advantage, popularity, agreeable company, pleasant travelling and friendships contributed useful experience for the future.

Some very impulsive, and expressive emotions, would have produced some hasty decisions, but if Gerald had kept from rash conduct, then he would have felt liberal and free, and would have had success through quick response, through mirth, cheerfulness and readiness to participate in pleasure and gaiety. This would have been a good time for mixing with others generally, and for sentimental, highly moral and idealistic feelings, but not so good a time, perhaps, for associations with women, causing unpopularity.

Friends: New friends were made, but separations occurred also. However, all matters connected with friendships would have been brought to the fore. He would have made new friends, or acquaintances, and have become closely associated with those that he considered to be his friends. Hence, Gerald's desires/ambitions for the future would have become stronger.

Family: Somewhat later, there may have been some family trouble, sadness/separation through friends and/or relatives, or some sort of disappointment, or anxiety caused through pleasures. But there would also have been a short, fortunate time for family, leading to benefit through Gerald's mother. Parenthood was denoted.

Lover: Love may have absorbed Gerald's senses, but there may have been trouble through his affection. Yet, conversely, conjugal ties, and secretive unions would have prospered.

Career

Early: This would have been a good time for coming before the public, and some new undertaking may have begun. There would have been more short journeys than formerly. There was public success, a good time for travelling and for moving home. Also, there would have been improved financial prospects and increased possessions. Gerald could have pushed his affairs to the front discreetly, but not in an undignified way. He may have undertaken a larger responsibility, but accompanied by some scandal, or financial loss, trouble through money, but adherence to contracts and opinions, would have proved profitable for the future. The more hope that he could have cultivated at this time, the more successful he would have become. He should have curbed his desires, and have sought to act temperately in all things, to keep himself from being called-out from his centre. If he had not balanced himself properly, then he may have done great harm to his future self-image and well-being. In the event, Gerald may have shown leadership of a dynamic kind, by keeping previous reservations in mind.

Middle: Gerald should have used his assertiveness carefully to get himself through any difficult/depressing times.

Charity: Gerald may have become more aware of charitable activities. His emotional state may well have become stirred favourably by the need for engaging in hidden charity. His good imagination would have become useful for charitable affairs.

Health

Gerald's health might have suffered when his mind became depressed. However, his health would have improved after a short while, but there may have been some temporary blood disorders, due to surfeit and excess bile.

— —

Gerald Ford Becoming Vice-President and President, October, 1973 to January, 1976, from his Epoch and Birth Charts, Secondary Progressions and Transits.

(see Figures 9 and 10)

Character

General: Some general benefit and success may have been had, resulting from a softening of Gerald's nature, together with an enhanced resistance to frustration. Concurrently, his will would have been strengthened, making it independent and authoritative. The time was good for stimulated, domestic affairs/changes, for home-life and for terminating important matters that had been awaiting settlement. There may have been some failure of undertakings, some confusion in matters of high ideals, and in long-distance affairs, i.e. complications abroad. Also, he may have become full of emotion, including love of the arts, coupled additionally with a love of beauty.

Mentality: By awakening the intellectual side of his nature, he would have benefitted greatly at this time. It was good for his mind generally, and so favourable for reading, study, education, literary work, lecturing and for making speeches. His mind would have become very intuitive, and so more than usually inclined to the philosophical, thereby tending to bring-out the inner part of his nature. Although his mind had been steadied, he may have become more liable to depression. Gravity of mind, and thoughtfulness would have induced an inclination to engage in profound studies. His artistic sensibilities would have been stimulated. He will have had the opportunity to investigate those things connected with aspirations and hopes, which were mental and spiritual, rather than physical and material. If he could have absorbed both expansion and contraction, and have blended these two, then his whole character would have been strengthened by steadfastness and perseverance. His mind would have become intensified in all matters connected with philosophy and religion. Also, Gerald would have developed his faculty for reading character, and for judging human nature.

Possibly, Gerald would have become attracted by occult phenomena. There may have been some psychic consciousness experienced. But the time was good for the psychic investigation of the sub-conscious. To the awakened, it may have brought reconciliation to a change of consciousness, and to thoughts about life-after-death. Possibly, he would have had some peculiar experiences, remarkable dreams, and out-of-body experiences while asleep. However, he must not have given way to fancy, and it would have been important for him to distinguish between the false and the true; and the real and the unreal. Any changes that did occur may have become accompanied by uncertainty, worry, indecision, unpopularity, disfavour and loss.

At this time, Gerald would have felt irritable, inclined to become excitable, and so easily provoked. His mind may have become sarcastic, with a lack of peaceful expression. Things may have appeared to be distorted, when viewed from the wrong standpoint, so that he should have been careful in all his dealings with others, especially with agents and 'cute' people, generally. Some quarrels and troubles may have cropped-up. Also, later, there may have been trouble with writing, solicitors, travel and relatives. Great caution would have been needed in making any speech. An unfavourable influence would have tended to make his mind over-sharp, i.e. too keen and alert, so that he would have over-reached himself in some way, perhaps over-stepping the bounds of moderation, and/ or of discretion. There may have been sudden reversals of ideas. Hence, there could have developed the danger of disrepute, quarrels with others, and aroused opposition. He should have avoided all correspondence and the signing of important papers, until his mind had settled, and he had 'seen' clearly, free from prejudice and bias. He may have become prone to worry, and have become overly anxious, seeing things in a jaundiced way, due partly to an over-wrought condition. Once again, he should have used great care in all the things that he did.

Later, there would not have been a favourable time mentally, tending to make his mind wayward, irritable and liable to be troublesome. His mind would have been over-active, impulsive and hasty. He could have been moody, idealistic, yielding and changeable. He may have felt that he was becoming isolated from other minds, and so vitally needing his own self-expression.

Yet energy would have been given for an inspired, always searching, and versatile, as well as original, sensational and revolutionary, mind-set. This would have been a good time for his mind, making it bright and cheerful. Later, his mind would have become sharpened, eager to learn and to gain experience. Energetic and industrious, he would have been very keen, shrewd and practical in all matters requiring mental ability. Also, there would have been an ability to put into practice, any latest ideas. He should have met with success in most of his activities, being able to observe accurately and quickly. Now would have been a good time for writing, and for dealings with agents and solicitors. In fact, it was favourable for peak experience, which he would have needed to make concrete through compulsion and sensitivity.

Lifestyle: A new cycle would have been brought into his life. Generally, he would have taken-on more refined and humane views, and to have tried to look at all things from a higher mental standpoint. However, there would have been a forcible separation of the thinking principle from habitual feelings, conventional thoughts, domestic customs and hidebound observances of all kinds. His feelings in his new expansiveness would have been at war with the fixed habit of thought, so that artistic enlightenment was likely to result at the cost of some sacrifice of any pedantic tendencies that there may have been in his disposition. This new cycle would have been brought into active expression, during which a more fixed and concentrated mentality would have been supplied, giving him more power to apply his mind to deeper studies. Because he was really progressive, he would have developed a keener interest to enter into the purely human side of his nature, and to have taken from it that part wherein the lower, or personal, mind, had a stronger voice than the higher, subjective one. He would have become more courageous, more enterprising, more competent and more adventurous than usual.

Relationships

Others: Gerald needed to be careful in his dealings with others. He would have been liable to suffer from deception at this time, and would have needed to watch all his affairs more carefully and minutely. He should have avoided contact with others. He would have suffered from ill-repute and personal attacks. He had to have guarded against any misunderstandings, and have dealt with everyone on an impartial and non-personal basis. On the other hand, his dealings with those who would have benefitted him both socially and financially, would have gone well. Once again, he would have had the ability to combine the methods of others, and to have added to them some distinctive factor of his own.

Gerald would have met persons who would have stirred him both mentally and physically, and whose influence upon his life would have been such as to make it active, bold, generous and free. He would have been likely to have given way to feelings, and to have formed attachments that would have been ardent, and eventful, while they lasted. But when they had subsided, he would have realised that he had been stirred into activity from the outside, i.e. more from the excitation of his desires, than from the energy of his inner will. This would have been an eventful period, which would have been remembered for years later. But one year later, he would have felt irritable, inclined to become excitable, and so easily provoked by others. He may have strongly, and even fanatically, resented their attitude towards himself. As a result, he should have been guarded in all his dealings with strangers, or with those with whom he had been brought into contact, accidentally, for he would have been liable to mis-representation and slander, or at the least, to very harsh criticism. His expression may have become nervous, and so he had to watch what he said and did, concerning others. But possibly, he could have regained some of his popularity by his ability to arouse mass emotions.

<u>Friends:</u> Gerald would have met fresh experience in connection with friends, some of whom would have played a very important part in his life history. But he could not have been too careful regarding the acquaintances that he cultivated now. This would have been a good time for binding and lasting social attachments, out of which many benefits would have been obtained. An emotional activity of a romantic attachment, with whom he would have had a karmic link, would have been apt to play an important part in his life, at this time, perhaps through some sort of marriage transformation.

New friends would have been very helpful and beneficial. Again, one year later, he would have been liable to disappointment between himself and his friends, and he should have acted as discreetly as possible. Friendship matters would have been brought to the fore. Gerald would have made new friends, or acquaintances, or have become closely associated with those whom he considered to be his friends. However, adverse influences would have required care regarding his friends, while favourable ones tended to help and provide success through dealings that came his way. He would have formed some very favourable, permanent attachments, ending in fruitful union. But there were separations, loss of friends and broken bonds. There was anxiety through friendships, with possible loss and disappointments, but he would have made fresh ones. Once again, there was loss through friends, treacherous enemies, opposition and disappointments. Gerald had a vital need for friendship, but he was able to influence his friends. There were mirthful and beneficial friends, as well as the loss of them. Possible disappointments in friendships, their losses and in social pleasures, may have led him to the danger of excesses.

<u>Family:</u> Gerald had a vital interest in relatives and neighbours. He would have had very pleasant dealings with kindred, or relatives. There was benefit through his wife, family and through domestic and social matters.

<u>Lover:</u> Attachments would have been of an idealistic, or mental, character. His affections could have become intensified. However, there was possible trouble of a romantic nature. He should have been

careful in his dealings with the opposite sex, whose influence on him could have become inimical. Possibly, platonic unions would have been formed.

Career

Early: Voyages were indicated along with a good time to travel, as well as for finance, tending to an increase of honour. There may have been some gain of money, benefit through superiors, or elders, and health. A change of occupation may have occurred with an increase in power and prominence. Group leadership of a dynamic kind could largely have hinged on a faculty for understanding group psychology, and upon a genius for persuasively exploiting his own personality. But a year later, it would have been a poor time for travel, or for making important changes, and, as always, he should have tried to keep himself as calm and as self-controlled as possible. There would have been enmity of superiors and from those in power. Much would have depended on his attitude towards his environment and surroundings, at the time. He needed to limit his force, and not give way to rash decisions. Some sort of brain condition, or eyesight trouble, may have impaired his executive ability during this time (July, 1974). But there was a favourable influence benefitting him financially. He should have gained honour and reputation, and should have risen to a more responsible and important position in life. This would have been a steadier period, in which improvement was made, and progress would have been of the honest type, which would have been so beneficial to his own individual character. Now foundation may have been laid for much future good. Somewhat later, there was a good time for honour, fortune and reputation. Fame and good report would have followed, such that his credit would have been strengthened. Also, there was gain possible through partners and co-workers. But the enmity of superiors, or that from those in power, would have continued. However, being intent on service, he would have mobilised his resources, but he would have needed to guard against unscrupulous employees/subordinates. There was sudden advancement to a powerful position, with success through originality.

There was a very favourable influence for enterprise, new ventures and all matters requiring independence of action. Gerald would have met with martial people, making him desire activity, adventure and risk. He would have been apt to busy himself in all directions with an alert mind, an inclination to travel and to make fresh outlets for his restless energies. He was active and progressive with executive faculties at their highest. A difficult influence, but of relatively short duration (one month) could have brought sorrow and trouble. He might have reacted impulsively, which would have reacted upon him, and have caused him to suffer. From January, 1975 there was an unfavourable time requiring him to keep travel to a minimum, and to keep as calm and quiet as he possibly could, but this could have led to a good time for terminating matters requiring settlement. However, there may have been failure of some undertakings, confusion in matters of high ideals, and in long-distance affairs, i.e. complications abroad.

Gerald showed desire to work with, or at the head of, a group. There were opportunities for making radical changes, and for obtaining completely fresh contacts and experiences. This would have been a time of many changes. There was a good possibility for a long voyage, some public favour and general financial benefit. However, there may have been a setback to prestige from an inability to work in harmony with others, including large organisations. But energy would have been provided for vital experiences, e.g. through travel. There may have been some indirect success from foes, or enemies, and so, often good following bad, or even poor, conditions. Also, the time was good for occultism, secret adventures and for unpopular enterprises. But there was a time for rest needed, and more attention for his household.

Vocation: Gerald developed an interest in healing, as a means of protecting loved ones.

Middle: Perhaps preparation for his retirement was started, as well as making sure of benefits for family and heirs. Gerald would have undergone a period of liability to suffer from much discredit, but with some compensation from mitigating circumstances. Also, unexpected changes could have proved beneficial.

Charity: Personal, charitable activities could have come to the fore. Thoughtful opposition to hidden charity would have started to recede. Charity may have been donated favourably to hidden (artistic) affairs, but with uncertainty, caution and with a steadying, as well as limiting, effect. Charity also began at home but more directly and decisively.

Health

Gerald's health could have been affected by a chilling and debilitating influence, so that he needed to keep cheerful and free from despondency. He needed to guard his health, and that of his family, in close connection, but there were improved conditions later. One year later, sudden and unexpected troubles could have arisen that would have been likely to affect his health by upsetting his nervous system. From January to April, 1974, there would have been periods when Gerald would have needed to safeguard his health from inflammatory, feverish complaints, from sensual problems and any experimentation with drugs should have been rigidly discountenanced. Gerald's health may have suffered from unusual diseases around June, 1975. Somewhat later, a favourable influence, strengthening his nervous system, would have made his mind bright, cheerful, keen and hopeful. But there would also have been lowered resistance, following-on from emotional distress. His interest in healing (see Vocation) would have been supported.

Figure 9: Secondary Progressions and Transits for PF becoming Vice-President on 13th October, 1973 from Epoch.

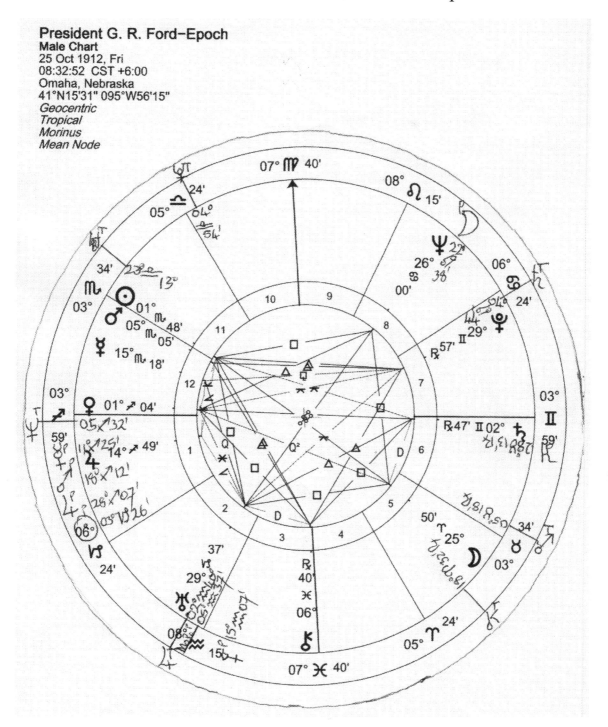

85

Figure 10: Secondary Progressions and Transits for PF Becoming Vice-President on 13th October, 1973, from Birth.

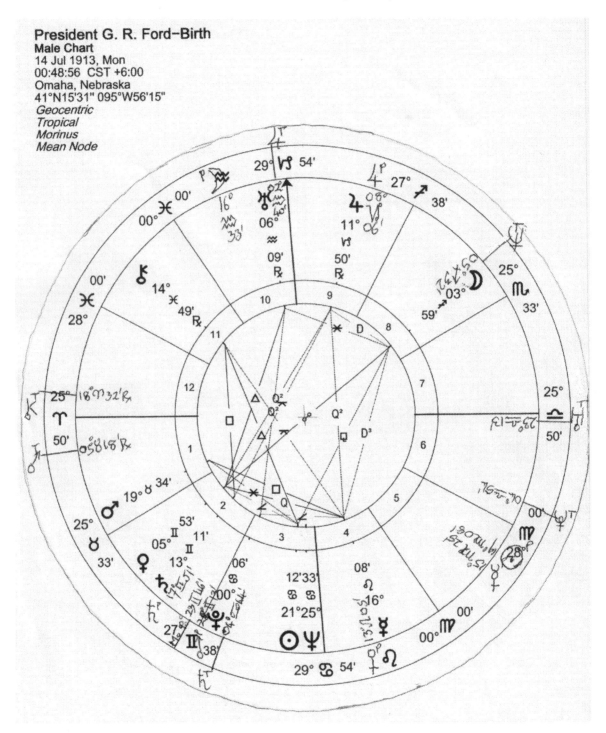

Gerald Ford's Death on the 26ᵗʰ December, 2006, at 18:45, Rancho Mirage, California. Secondary Progressions and Transits from his Epoch and Birth Charts.

'He made a far better President, than he did a Presidential Candidate.'
James Cannon

Character

General: This would have been a bad time for engagements. There could have been changes in his home-life, including removal to a distance, so that there may well have been trouble through his household, through home and as well as through property. Gerald would have had to stay cheerful, hopeful and patient. On the other hand, Gerald's will-power would have been strengthened and he would have been given more determination and purpose than usually, but there would have been various disappointments for him to contend with.

Mentality: Gerald should have avoided worry, becoming overly anxious and brooding. When irritable, he may have had inordinate desires. A frittering away of his energy would have weakened his sagacity, and his enthusiasm, creating a feeling of impotence. Also, dealing with correspondence would have interfered with his peace-of-mind, because he felt likely to have been misunderstood, thereby leading to misconceptions. But with patience, all this would have passed.

There may have been consolidation, due to a change of consciousness, involving thought about life-after-death, a desire to meditate and to think deeply. Confusion in his mind may have led to its wandering. His mind would neither have been over-cheerful, nor would any matters relating to pleasures, society or entertainments have been negotiated successfully.

All matters connected with his personality would have come to the fore, and much would have depended upon his own actions, his own attitude of mind and on how he would have been affected, but there could well have been changes of opinion and habits of mind, but troubles through writing. Some of these could have been desirable, so that he didn't have to fight them all!

There may have been some peculiar and weird happenings, remarkable dreams and out-of-body experiences, while asleep. He would have become impressionable, so that he must not have given way to anything that went against his common-sense, or outraged his reason, because it would have been important for him to be able to distinguish between the false and the true, and the real and the unreal. This would not have been a favourable influence by any means. But later, dreams, the psychic and the subconscious side of his nature would have been favoured. These may possibly have led to some religious experience and/or a peaceful death. He may have become idealistic, with a vital interest in philosophy, religion, or with an urge to expand his knowledge.

However, another influence would have tended to bring some worry and anxiety, especially with regard to finance and general affairs. He would have become somewhat depressed, inclined to despondency and to have looked on the black side of things. Disappointments may well have occurred, but in the end would have proved to be of only a trifling character. On the other hand, his mind would have expanded, and have become hopeful, bright and intelligent. He would have become more intuitive, would have had good judgement and would have been able to arrange his affairs satisfactorily. Correspondence, journeys and influential people would have benefitted him. He would have become more interested in philosophy, religion and higher subjects to his future advantage. Generally, this could have become a very good period. Mentally, he could have become more active and alert than usual, especially concerning general conditions. There could have been some gain through enterprise, or through the deaths of others, or from those with whom his life had been bound-up in any way.

Lifestyle: There would have been some trouble. Gerald would have become over-anxious and inclined to worry. He would have been brought into the gloomier, more brooding and melancholic side of his nature, which would have made him more liable to give way to depression. He had to have fought this with a firm will, for he would have had many experiences that would have been far from pleasant, and have come into contact with persons whose influence would not have been beneficial. He may have become a keen lover of animals, or dumb life, which would have caused an awakening of deeper sympathies, with a desire to help all those who suffer. He may well have become more hospitable, with a far wider sympathy for others than formerly. This would not have been a fortunate period and may have brought sorrow and some confinement, which would have been imposed upon him by circumstances, for a hampering, or restrictive influence of some kind, there was sure to be.

[N.B. The year that lay ahead would not have been that eventful, because the progressed Sun would not have met any aspects during its progress through the Epoch horoscope. On the other hand, lunar influences may have become more noticeable, but progressions in general, would have become more restricted in scope.]

An influence on Gerald's life may have been manifested in its physical expression, because it would have been more likely to have been felt internally and psychically, rather than outwardly. He would have become very receptive, but far more negative, than usual, so that he would have received vibrations from without to such an extent as to make him painfully sensitive to his environment and general surroundings. Although feelings and emotional affairs would have suffered, causing the severance of existing ties, loss of friends and those to whom he was deeply attached (under a separate influence) care would have been necessary in dealing with those who had had a share in his affections. Care would also have been needed with regard to monetary interests, lest losses of affection, or of property, had occurred under this unfavourable vibration. But Gerald would have been able to sense the conditions of others, and to have felt them in a peculiar way, so that he could have found himself unusually hospitable, sympathetic and even timid.

As a progressive, Gerald would have been given the opportunity to taste of that universal love, which is free from personal taint, but this touch of the 'universal solvent' comes only to those who are very advanced.

Relationships

Others: Gerald would have needed to be very careful in all his dealings with others. He would have been liable to suffer from some deception under this influence, so that he should have watched his affairs carefully and minutely. Additionally, there would have been troubles through women, and there may even have been trouble through children.

Friends: Matters concerning friendship would have been brought to the fore. He may have found himself deserted by those he had trusted in. However, friends were formed among those interested in the occult, but other friends could have been lost through disagreements, or separations. Gerald was inclined to demand too much of friendship, but he also did have a wide circle of artistic and intuitive friends. As a result, his desires would have become stronger, and the more hope that he could have cultivated, the more successful he would have become.

Family: This may not have been a good time for dealings with kindred, or relatives, and there may have been disputes with them.

Lover: There would have been prudence in affection.

Career

Early: This was a bad time for dealing with elders, or with those in responsible posts, and poor for any enjoyments. Financial considerations would have dominated his outlook. Gerald may have been deceived in his speculations and disappointed in his hopes. Generally, clerks, servants, messengers, or agents would have been the source of trouble. There may have been extravagance, or loss, and trouble through law and religion.

A further influence would have brought some connection with hospitals, or institutions, into his life, possibly for the first time, and perhaps for some temporary confinement, either through ill health, or other unavoidable cause. A further influence would have brought delay, or loss, in connection with his affairs. His public position, or reputation, may have suffered with a loss of credit, the disfavour of superiors, and sorrow through friends. This would have been an unfavourable and unpleasant influence. In addition, there would have been financial loss, coupled with domestic afflictions, sorrows and disappointments. On the other hand, there was the possibility of a long sea voyage, with some public favour, general gain and attachments of a somewhat successful character.

Gerald should have made the very most of a favourable period financially, socially and affectionately. This good influence could have marked an important stage in his development. For completeness, there could have been some troubles while travelling, with home, property, investments and elders, which would have required careful examination, as well as possible loss through religion, philosophy and law. But increased power may have developed.

Charity: Gerald's mind may have become sarcastic, regarding philanthropy/charity, and especially in regard to home, domestic and family affairs. But he did have a charitable mind, even though with limitation. However, there was possible expansion of charity in home affairs, but with difficulty. Alternatively, Gerald may have become eager to learn about all charitable affairs. He may have had latent charitable ideas, which he could have put into practice. For example, there could have been more care and thought concerning the welfare of the young, leading to an enhanced reputation. There would have been originality to accompany his charitable dealings.

Health

At this time, Gerald's health tended to suffer through a lack of vitality, and through depletion, even though his health may have received vigour and increased vitality. His circulation may have become slower than usual. There may have been deep-seated, functional disorders. A strong influence would have tended to lessen, or disorganise, his vitality, thereby destabilising his health. Additionally, his vitality would have been rundown by a further, but relatively short-term (one month) influence, making him prone to colds, chills and depressed circulation. His teeth and digestive system may have needed sustaining against the effects of over-anxiety, during this time. Moreover, there may have been difficulties with his generative system. Assertive persons could have caused disputes, leading to feverish problems, accompanied by tendencies to upset his nerves. He should have tried to avoid them.

— —

Tertiary Progressions and Transits for Gerald Ford's Death on 26th Dec. 2006, at 18:45, in Rancho Mirage, California, from his Epoch and Birth Charts.

Character

General: There was an unfavourable period containing disappointments. Neither cheerfulness, nor any pleasures, society or entertainments would have been negotiated successfully. But there was some force added to Gerald's character. His desire for action and impulse would have been stimulated. He had to have reined-in excess of force, which would have caused him to act impulsively, hastily and rashly. His lower nature would have proved difficult to control and manage, but only on account of the excess force that the influence generated. He should have avoided travel. Obstinacy, self-will and firmness could have been turned into determination and strength of purpose. He should have tried to make the most of his personal abilities. There would have been changes in his life, and possibly, trouble through sudden ones. But a fortunate time for domestic affairs would have enabled Gerald to enter into a happy and pleasurable period. His whole nature would have felt expanded.

Mentality: Gerald's critical, and somewhat selfish style, would have become softened, bringing more intuition and receptivity into his life. Gravely and seriously disposed, he would have been able to criticise and analyse all things – including himself. His mind would have become more active, original, keen, alert and eager to be busy. He would have become more solid, practical and discriminating. He may well have shown consideration, thoughtfulness and method. His memory should have become good. Also, he would have learned the value of concentration, for dissipation over a thousand different objects is merely energy wasted. He may well have become inclined to take-on laborious, painstaking and industrious tasks, i.e. great undertakings. Indeed, he would have been responsive to all improvements. Also, there would have been opportunity to improve his mind, as well as improvements in his agility and quickness, e.g. have shown more prudence in speech and conduct. True obedience, i.e. a combination of love and intellect, may have been experienced. Thus, he may have worked solely for the love of it, rather than from any self-motive.

Now he would have arrived at a time during which a struggle would have taken place between his soul and his senses. He would have met both opportunities and disappointments. He would have become torn between will and desire, and will have found himself severely tried and tempted, but his actions now would have influenced his future destiny. He should have acted discreetly, and have been careful. This would have been 'a dangerous period'.

Also, deceit and fraud was possible, as well as a lack of trust/ integrity. His vivid imagination would have involved uncommon relatives and neighbours. There may have been trouble through a love of fantasy, intensified sensitivity, fulfilment seeking, and writing. His nervous forces would have been quickened, rendering him alert and sprightly. Having been stimulated mentally, he had to have avoided becoming too expressive and overly zealous. He may have become overly enthusiastic, and have reacted with rash speech. He should have avoided legal affairs at this time. Possibly, he would have had a religious experience.

Lifestyle: There were no interpretations found for this section.

Relationships

Others: He would have contacted others, who could have influenced his life greatly, but no ties should have been formed (while the progressed Moon made afflicting influences with the other planets). Gerald had to have avoided 'hard' persons, and he had to have been careful in whom he put his trust, but support would have been given to reforms for the good of others. However, any personal gain would have been at others' expense.

There would have been activity in social affairs, and success through them, but he would have needed care regarding the welfare of the young, and there was possible trouble through children.

Friends: Gerald formed many new friends, and so had much social activity. However, he tended to demand too much of friends, but a wide circle of artistic, and possibly magnetic friends, was available. There were disagreements, separation and trouble through friends and acquaintances; all leading to sorrow and loss through them.

Family: Gerald made unfavourable contacts with female relations, and he became emotional regarding children and pleasure generally. Ties were severed, there was family trouble, and grief was likely.

Lover: Dealings with the opposite sex could have proved inimical. But there was prudence in affection. He could have given vent to ardent emotions, along the lines of least resistance. Gerald's emotions suffered, but were awakened in terms of love affairs. Yet there was a tendency to bring a separation between himself and someone else, to whom he was much attached.

Career

Early: There was an unpleasant influence regarding finance and the loss of money; there were domestic afflictions as well as sorrow and disappointments. Gerald's progress would have been retarded and his actions limited, both of which would have depressed him. He needed to order his affairs with care. As a result, concentrated concerns over finance would have dominated his outlook. There wold have been some success through business, but also loss of business, of property, and in domestic matters. Travel and document signing would not have been favoured during this time.

Yet Gerald would have shown more practical ability either for business, or profession, for special work, or for general industry. There could have been an opportunity for entering a new phase, perhaps intensely.

Later, financial prospects should have improved, and there would have been opportunities to bring monetary affairs into a better condition than formerly, according to his financial ability. Now, would have been a good time to engage in investment. Improved financial conditions and otherwise, were likely. However, if stressful events had occurred, then care would have been necessary as appropriate, but with good influences, investment and speculation would go well. A further, favourable influence, inclined to improved monetary affairs, and gain through superiors, would have led-on to general improvements. But a very favourable influence denoting financial gain, would have followed.

There may have been some public recognition. When accompanied by other good influences, this would mark a very useful period. There would have been distinction in his position, and financial gain, but conversely, a liability to suffer lack of trust, and/or integrity in his subordinates/inferiors. On the other hand, there may have been disputes with superiors, and with those in authority, which would have resulted in loss of favour, and decline in reputation, but not too seriously.

Gerald could have gained in connection with sickness and nursing, or with regard to health matters generally. He would have enquired about laws of hygiene, food reform, or about physical health and fitness.

Vocation, Middle and Late: No interpretations were found for inclusion in these sections.

Charity: Gerald was concerned with philanthropy for the general public. He would have shown a lack of charity, and limitation of it. But there would have been unusual and sudden charity given, at this time, e.g. apparent rash action with intangible charity in the arts.

Health

Gerald had to guard against chills and poor circulation. This may have been the beginning of other things to come, affecting his health, surroundings and environment. Gerald needed to safeguard his health, because there had been a change in his system, not helped by poor digestion, poor emotional state and worry.

A short-term influence did arise, which could have proved helpful to him, if he had been attempting some physical regeneration. He needed to stop any waste, any emotional expenditure, and have acted temperately, as well as minimising his diet. There would have been the possibility of good health, increased vitality and renewed vigour. He needed all this to make the most of his personal abilities. The problem was that if his health had suffered, then his mind was prone to become depressed.

Gerald should have watched his health when he was liable to inflammatory and feverish complaints. He needed to avoid hazards and to have guarded against troubles with his nerves. Going to extremes could have led to accidents, or violence. However, an influence fortunate for health, would have increased Gerald's vitality and bodily energy. It would have bestowed additional power on him, so that he could have coped with ordinary, occupational responsibilities, and/or undertakings.

— — — — — — — — — — — — — — — — — — — —

CHAPTER 10

Assessment of Prediction Groups.

It seems clear that the interpretations gathered for the tertiary progressions don't accord with PF's time of life, i.e. close to the end of it, whereas those for the secondary progressions do. As a result, for the following examples of forwards astrology of Oliver Strate, we shall just use the interpretations of Secondary Progressions and Transits as the 'method of choice' for prediction.

Because we are about to embark upon 'Forwards Astrology' for the first time, we need to consider the various groups of Prediction, which is the object of this book, by the 'method of choice', i.e. Secondary Predictions and Transits, and so get an idea of how they relate to each other. Normally, the future trend of a client's life, is of more interest to a client, than is that client's character portrait, even though the former is very much affected by the latter.

Firstly, we take the position of the progressed Morin Point, by the decanate of the Zodiacal sign that it occupies. Each sign of the zodiac comprises 30^0, which is divided into 3 equal parts of 10^0 each, called decanates. Consider Aries, the first sign. Its first decanate is the pure one, because Aries is the first sign of the fiery triplicity, so that we have Aries the sign combined with Aries of the triplicity. The second decanate of Aries we shall label as Aries – Leo, because Leo is the second sign of the fiery triplicity. Similarly, we label the third decanate of Aries as the Aries – Sagittarius decanate, because Sagittarius is the third sign of the fiery triplicity. The next sign is Taurus comprising three decanates of the earthy triplicity, namely Taurus, Virgo and Capricorn. Now, taking a leap, we realise that there are 36 different decanates altogether. Because the Morin Point progresses by about 1^0 for each year of life, we realise that each decanate corresponds to 10 years of a person's life. Thus, 3 signs will cover the whole range of a person's life of 90 years. We could assess each decanate's influence on a life by examining its major traits, and so become able to estimate how positive, negative or neutral its influence will be, when occupied by the progressed Morin Point. Normally, we can just look up the interpretations for each decanate, as given by a notable astrologer, e.g. Alan Leo.

Progressed aspects, to and from the Morin Point, as well as from the centre of the 10th House (near the M.C.) can be of some importance.

Our 2nd group of predictive interpretations comes from Solar progressions. We can imagine that the Sun is the short-hand of a clock, i.e. mainly the hour when progressions become due. The Moon tends to be the long-hand, pointing to the minute when the Sun's influence will operate. Solar progressions/aspects/influences operate over, or during, a period of 3 years, i.e. 18 months before becoming exact, and for 18 months after exactness. On the other hand, lunar progressions/aspects/influences operate only for about 1 month, i.e. for 2 weeks either side of exactness. Solar influences are vital, while lunar influences comprise a focus for solar influences.

Here, we shall consider only the influence of aspects formed between the progressed position of the Sun with the radical (root) of the planet in question, either at Epoch, or at Birth. We shall not consider, as a first approximation, aspects formed between two progressed planets, converse aspects (going backwards in time, rather than forwards), symbolic aspects (O-Ds) [every planet is progressed by 1^0 for each year of life], or aspects formed by alignment of planetary declinations by conjunction or opposition. Much depends upon the sign and House of participating planets at Birth, and/or at Epoch.

Our 3rd group of predictive interpretations concerns mutual progressions, i.e. aspects formed between progressed 'personal' planets, namely Mercury, Venus and Mars, with radical planets only, both at Birth and at Epoch. Mutual aspects of Mercury and Venus operate for about 1 year either side of exactness, but because Mars moves more slowly, then mutual aspects of Mars can last for up to 2 years either side of exactness.

Generally, progressions of 'generation' planets, namely from Jupiter to Pluto inclusive, are not considered, but there are times when Jupiter, and perhaps Saturn, progressed, can form significant aspects with radical planets, late in the lives of older people.

If any planet becomes Stationary, which is not possible for either the Sun, or Moon, from either apparent direct, or retrograde, motion, then, because its motion is much slowed, its influence will be longer, and stronger.

Our 4th group of predictive interpretations comes from aspects formed by the progressed Moon, with a person's radical/natal planets. While the Sun progresses by 1^0 through the zodiac for every year, the Moon progresses by 13^0 on average. Lunar aspects operate for one month roughly. However, aspects formed by the progressed Moon do have their own interpretations, but the strength of an influence, can depend on the concurrent aspects of the Sun. As indicated, progressed lunar aspects can act as a 'trigger' for progressed, solar aspects to operate.

Our 5th group of predictive interpretations concerns aspects formed by transiting planets with natal ones. These can be considered to be a day-for-a-day progressions. The duration of a transiting aspect, as is usual, is taken from the time when an aspect is within 1^0 of exactness. Thus, the period lasts, according to the apparent speed of the transiting planet.

Actual movement in the ephemeris is now being considered. When a transiting planet, say today, for example, is found to be in a degree which aspects a planet in a person's Epoch, or Birth, chart, then we state that that planet transits by conjunction, opposition, etc. to that person's natal planet. But, in fact, it would only be in such a relationship to that planet, many years ago, at the person's epoch, or birth. Without question, the transits of a planet are of the nature of that specific planet, and of the nature of the planet being transited in the natal chart. Earlier, we have said that a person's character is given in part, by the interpretation of the planet in that person's natal chart. Hence, the transit of a planet today, appears to stimulate that which is already an essential part of the person's character.

Transits of the Moon are extremely short, but those of the Sun last for about 3 days overall. Transits of Mercury and Venus will remain within 1^0 for no more than a day, while those of the slower Mars, can last for 3 – 4 days, stationary conditions excepted. However, the duration of transiting 'generation' planets, increases with the slowness of their apparent motions, so that the outermost ones may affect a life for weeks, when forming an aspect to an important degree in a natal chart. For Mars, only transits by conjunction will be considered; for

Jupiter and Saturn, only transits by conjunction and opposition will be considered; while transits by all four angles, i.e. 0^0, 90^0, 120^0 and 180^0, should prove more significant for the outer planets, namely Uranus, Neptune and Pluto.

To make sure that we spot all the lunar progressions, as well as all the required transits, it helps to tabulate them month by month, of the year to follow. Thus, across a table, we have the headings for columns of 'Date', 'Lunar Position', 'Progressed Lunar Aspects' and 'Transits'. The heading of the last, large column is then subdivided into six, namely 'Pluto', 'Neptune', 'Uranus', 'Saturn', 'Jupiter', and 'Mars', and then the Table is filled-in, as required. Astrologers also add a column headed 'New Moons', i.e. for double transits of the Sun and Moon, but we are trying to keep things 'Simple'.

Finally, our 6th group comprises the interpretations for the sign and House positions of the progressed Moon (see A. Leo and M. E. Hone). Incidentally, we can use the accepted abbreviations for the planets and for the types of aspect. We can also use the abbreviations for the states of the planets. Thus subscript 'r' stands for radical, 'p' stands for progressed, while 't' stands for transiting.

— —

Now let us begin our task by taking a cursory look at Oliver Strate's natal charts. Here we have a situation that closely resembles that of Queen Mary. We see that Oliver's Morin Point at Epoch and at Birth both lie in the 2nd Aries decanate, and are just under 1^0 apart. This means that his progressed charts tend to follow each other, which will simplify interpretations. Also, we see that his Moon at Epoch is conjoint the Morin Point, while his Morin Point at Birth, opposes it. This is a consequence of applying the rules of the Pre-Natal Epoch, but, once again, this tends to ease the process of our prediction exercise. Because the two Morin Points both lie in the 2nd Aries decanate (Mars is the chart ruler and the Sun is the decanate ruler) Mars and the Sun are important planets for Oliver throughout his life. At Epoch, the planet Mars lies in Leo (ruled by the Sun), and is almost a singleton. It lies at the focus of the chart (many of the aspects in the chart point towards Mars) and somewhat unusually its motion is retrograde. We see that the Sun itself lies in Capricorn and that it forms a sesquiquadrate (an unfavourable, but fairly weak) aspect with Mars. We note that Saturn is the ruler of the Sun in Capricorn, and that it is occupied by Libra, wherein it is exalted. However, it is in poor (square) aspect to the Sun, and is semi-square to Mars. The planets Jupiter, Neptune and Chiron all oppose Mars, but this situation is mitigated somewhat by Mars being in trine to the Moon, which it rules. We have a sextile between Uranus and Mercury, and we see that Chiron, in its planetary group, is bi-semi-sextile to Uranus and Mercury. Have we now formed some sort of feeling for Oliver's Epochal chart?

At birth, we see that, once again, the chart ruler is Mars, that the Sun in Libra is ruled by Venus, which is conjoint Mars, and which is also stationary. We see that the Moon, opposite the Morin Point, is conjoint the Sun, that is weakly conjoint with Saturn (exalted in Libra) that, in turn, is strongly conjoint Mercury, all four planets being in Libra in the 7th House. As at birth, Pluto lies in Capricorn (ruled by Saturn) in the 10th House, and is bi-square to Uranus and Mercury. There are four, if not five, groups of closely conjoint planets in his birth chart, four planets of which are in retrograde motion. Again, have we formed some sort of feeling for Oliver's birth chart?

— — — — — — — — — — — — — — — — — — — —

CHAPTER 11

Forwards Astrology 1

Oliver Strate

Oliver's character portrait is given in Appendix 3, coupled with his natal charts at the end of it (see figures 5 and 6). Because we have no idea of what Oliver's main life events will be, or when they will occur, we have taken roughly three progressed Moon journeys, in turn, as examples, around the horoscope/zodiac. We hope that this too, will simplify interpretations. Hence, we shall be examining his situation after 28 years, after 56 years and after 84 years. Figures 11 and 12 present the Epoch and Birth charts for prediction for the last case (see the end of this chapter). Let us take a cursory look at these two charts:-

Both charts consist of 3 concentric circles, as in the previous two cases of QM and PF. From Epoch, we see that the progressed Morin Point lies in Cancer's 1st decanate, in the 4th House, the progressed Sun has entered the 1st House, at the end of Pisces, and the progressed Moon lies in Taurus, just in the 3rd decanate, in the 2nd House. The progressed Mercury and Venus both lie in the 1st House, and the progressed Mars has just entered Leo at the end of the 4th House. Although the progressed Jupiter has moved through half a sign (15°) it makes no major aspect with the planets at Epoch, and the progressed Saturn has not yet moved through 3° apparently. Interestingly, there is a group of three transiting planets, i.e. Neptune, Chiron and Mars, that have entered the 6th House, in Virgo. Transiting Saturn is conjoint the Epochal Mars, and transiting Uranus is about to start passing through the 1st House. The progressed Sun is square to the Epochal Venus; the progressed Mercury opposes the Epochal Saturn, and the progressed Venus will be in trine to the Epochal Mars, in a few years' time. Examples of the progressed Moon aspects include a trine to the Epochal Mercury, a square to the Epochal Jupiter and a quincunx to the Epochal Sun, but all these, at different times throughout the year.

From Birth, we see that the progressed Morin Point lies in the 1st Cancer decanate in the 4th House, just as for the Epoch case. The progressed Sun in Capricorn in the 10th House is square to Saturn at Birth, and the progressed Venus in Scorpio in the 8th House has become semi-square to Mercury at Birth, while the progressed Mars in Capricorn resides in the 10th House. The progressed Moon lies in Scorpio in the 8th House and is about to become conjoint with Venus at Birth, followed then by Mars at Birth. Later in the year, it will become trine to Jupiter, and then to Uranus. The progressed Mercury in Sagittarius occupies the 9th House. Transiting Uranus has passed over the Jupiter – Uranus conjunction at Birth, but may return there by virtue of retrograde motion later on.

But firstly, let us read the completed prediction for Oliver's situation after the first cycle of the progressed Moon, which occurred before his 30th birthday. Similarly, and following on, we have presented the completed predictions for the end of Oliver's second and third cycles of the progressed Moon. At least, we now have some idea of what future prediction is like.

Interpretations of Secondary Progressions and Transits for the end of Oliver Strate's First Period, 2038 – 9 A.D.

Character

General: Oliver's responses will become more possessive, with a keen liking for the good things of the earth (09/38 – 06/39). Domesticity, health matters and life generally will proceed favourably (for 2 weeks either side of 11/12/2038). A good influence will stimulate Oliver's emotions and sensibilities (for 2 weeks either side of 20/10/2038). New undertakings may make this a busy period for him, but it just may only indicate agility, quickness and mental alertness (for 2 weeks either side of 11/10 2039). A further weak influence will operate, in many ways favourably, because it will steady and quieten his whole nature, making opportunities for thrift, economy and carefulness (for 2 weeks either side of 09/11 2039). However, an unfavourable influence does not help travel, important changes, or discretion, so that he should try to keep as calm and as self-controlled as possible (for 6 weeks either side of 12/02/2039). This period could prove trying.

Around 07/10/2038, Mars transits by conjunction the position of the progressed Moon, in Libra, in the 7th House, as well as do Jupiter by sextile, Saturn by semi-sextile and Pluto by trine. These transits cannot be strong, or long-lasting, but briefly Oliver might expect generosity, energy, steadiness and intensity to accompany his gentle, companionable and diplomatic responses.

Mentality: Oliver will become more a) discriminating, b) critical, c) intuitive and d) perceptive. Matters requiring these four traits to become active, will engage his attention from 3 years ago until 9 years hence. Intellectual psychic affairs may attract him, but the best attributes of this time, of solidity, practicality and discernment will now be available to him. However, he will need to guard against becoming too harassed and distressed by petty restrictions that may cause him some sorrow and annoyance. In addition, a slightly more negative influence will cause his mind to look upon life in a more grave and steady mood (for 2 weeks either side of 27/12/38). Indeed, simultaneously, Oliver's mind may have become more suspicious lately, and he may have become more inclined to look upon the dark side of things (10/37 to 10/39). He may oscillate between two courses, namely between uncertainty and with the best course of action to take (between 04/38 and 12/39). Also, he may become disappointed by sudden estrangements, money losses and downturns in business affairs (08/39 to 10/41).

On the other hand a new experience, of a psychic nature, may bring him in touch with impressions connected to higher states of consciousness because his mind will be very sensitive. There can be a peculiar charm about Neptune experiences (for 2 weeks either side of 08/01/39).

Lifestyle: Oliver will show sympathy and affection to all those in close contact. This will help his prospects to become brighter and happier than for some time. Indulgence in pleasure, and in the pursuit of happiness, coupled with his cheerful side, will make him more hopeful, congenial and friendly. This particular influence could prove splendid for cultivating his feelings and his higher emotions (04/38 – 04/41).

Saturn is the planet of refinement, chastity and temperance, and by studying the virtues of purity, industry, patience and perseverance, distinct progress would be made (11/38 – 11/41).

Relationships

Others: Oliver may form helpful contacts as the result of his cheerful and adaptable frame of mind (for 2 weeks either side of 20/11/38).

Friends: There may be opportunities to make general improvements, in which Oliver will find joy and pleasure in new friends (for 2 weeks either side of 11/12/38).

Family: There may be some misfortune, or loss, in his family circle (07/38 – 10/39), which he will feel keenly. There could be some sorrow, or disappointment, through separation (10/37 – 10/39).

Lover: There could be a new accentuation of the male principle in his life (for 15 months either side of 08/38, i.e. from 05/37 – 12/39). Strange attachments may arise, in which magnetic influence plays a prominent part, but none of this will be too serious, but Oliver nevertheless, should be forewarned about any unfavourable conditions that may occur (09/38 – 08/40).

Some young woman of a karmic kind may play an important role in his life at this time (for 2 weeks either side of 20/11/38). However, he should be on guard generally, when dealing with the opposite sex, with expenditure, waste and any excess of anxiety (for 2 weeks either side of 09/10/39).

Success in attachments/marriage is indicated for 12 months either side of 08/38). A further, strong influence often indicates marriage – light and life are connected with all harmony and unison (from 04/38 – 04/41). Oliver will now be brought into contact with others, who will influence his life greatly. He may well enter partnerships, unions, marriage and association with others, if this is done while the progressed Moon forms a favourable aspect with any other planet, which is not itself afflicted, namely, its trine to Venus radical, (see his Epoch chart) i.e. two weeks either side of 20th Sept. 2038. Yet another, weak influence, may affect him only indirectly, during which magnetic relationships of attraction will cause him to act by impulse, rather than with discretion (for 2 weeks either side of 12/02/2039). There is also the transient expectation that his marriage partner will be motherly (09/38 – 11/38).

Career

Early: There will be practical capability and connection with sickness, nursing and health matters. He will become more interested in hygiene and bodily welfare (for 7 – 9 more years). He may become stimulated to show and gain recognition for his abilities. Things will solidify and become more permanent. His honour and reputation may profit, there may be some gain through government (11/37 – 11/40) and influential people could mould his future onto a firmer basis (05/38 – 05/41).

Additionally, matters connected with finance will come to the fore. A weak, although unfavourable influence, may denote some financial difficulties, discredit, loss of friends or reputation, through others, elders and those in authority. He should keep his mind free from worries, and not become depressed (between 10/37 – 10/39). During this period he should guard against theft and fraud, as well as cultivate hope and cheerfulness to counter any despondency encountered.

Financially, a favourable outcome could occur (from 11/38 – 01/39). This could prove to be a good time for inspiration, or imagination, which could prove beneficial for historical authors, for example. However, Oliver may need to be careful regarding money-seeking ways. A good time could now mark an epoch in his life. His feelings and emotions should find a very satisfactory outlet, leading to a welcome result. This could be a good time for pleasure, sociability, advancement and prosperity. He should try to make the most of the opportunity presented (for 2 weeks either side of 20/09/2038). Also, he may develop any latent ability to undertake any creative, artistic work (for 2 weeks either side of 20/11/2038). Moreover, he may enter a period of success, realising ambitions, hopes and wishes (for 2 weeks either side of 11/12/2038). Another, weak influence may be good for financial and social matters. He should push his affairs, and busy himself while it operates (for 2 weeks either side of 10/01/2039). There is a further indication that changes in occupation, or habits, will prove beneficial, and that coming before the public, and/or the many, or making a journey, would be good also (for 2 weeks either side of 22/08/2039). In addition, there could be some chance of public favour and general gain (for 2 weeks either side of 18/09/2039).

A short period (from 29/09/2038 – 18/10/2038) may see a pre-occupation with the more serious side of life, resulting in prudent forethought and careful attention to details. But some benefit could result, e.g. an increase of power, or prominence, or attraction to things occult. Alternatively, sudden change in unusual, unobtrusive matters, or in quiet, but 'different' ways, could prove troublesome (for two weeks either side of 21/09/2038).

Vocation: Although generally, the period between 10/37 and 10/39, may be poor for writing, it could lead to improved monetary prospects. New undertakings may make this a busy period (for 2 weeks either side of 11/10/2039).

Middle: As a reformer, the influence (for 2 weeks either side of 12/02/2039) may prove beneficial, but he must not destroy before there could have been an opportunity to create renewal. His 'root of merit' (his inventiveness mainly) may be involved in this. His domestic instincts and his urge to get to the root of things, may enable him to make radical changes usefully, thereby gaining public popularity through his ability to arouse mass emotions (for 11 weeks centred on the 25/06/2039).

Dealings with the elderly, those with responsibility, and perhaps involving his own increased responsibility, will promote much thought, prudence and management of his affairs. This period (for 2 weeks either side of 09/11/2039) could well be used more for reflection rather than for any special efforts in the direction of external activities.

Charity: Four planetary transits to Chiron [from Mars, Jupiter, Saturn and Pluto] suggest that humanitarian, charitable affairs will become energised, expanded, canalised and intensified. Hopefully, they will be made benevolently (for a short time around 07/10/2038). There is a good period for charitable affairs, which will enable Oliver to display as much talent for charity, as he has latent within him (for 12 weeks centred on 12/01/2039).

Health

Oliver's health tends to become improved for the period 11/37 – 11/40. However, another influence may cause his health to suffer through affected circulation. Moderation in all things should help him to counter this (10/37 – 10/39). Additionally, sudden and unexpected troubles may affect his nervous system (during 08/38 – 06/40). He may become irritable, excitable and easily provoked, thereby offending others, or resenting their attitude towards himself. Also, he should avoid becoming cold, i.e. he needs to keep his circulation in good order, and generally keep his system, as a whole, well nourished (between 10/37 – 10/39).

Vitality, bodily energy and additional power to cope in general should be available between 02/38 – 02/40. However, Oliver should keep himself in shape, neither becoming too depressed, nor fretting excessively, as these latter will retard his progress and delay his affairs (for 2 weeks either side of 27/12/2038). On the other hand, his health, home and general affairs should be supported (for 2 weeks either side of 22/08/2039).

Interpretations of Secondary Progressions and Transits for the end of Oliver Strate's Second Period, 2066 – 7 A.D.

Character

General: There will have been an on-going influence, which will be weakening slowly to nothing for the next eighteen months. Within this time there may have been setbacks due to rash, or unrestrained, action. There may have been changes in his habits, in domestic affairs and in social concerns, but it may not have been a favourable time for him to become too involved in any of these things. Although Oliver's domestic instincts, and his urge to get to the root of things, may be stimulated (for two weeks either side of 05/12/2066, and for 2 weeks either side of 24/01/2067) some extreme rashness, or great trouble from an unexpected quarter, could stress his feelings to the extent that he will require all the self-control that he can muster, to contend with it. This will be a 'dangerous' influence, controllable only by the power of his own spirit (from 03/67 to 09/70). On the other hand, a weak, but favourable influence could steady and quieten his whole nature (for 2 weeks either side of 20/03/2067). Later on, a weak, unfavourable influence will require Oliver to be on guard against impulsiveness, irritability and abruptness (for 2 weeks either side of 30/03/2067 and again for 19/07/2067). But a favourable, weak influence (for 2 weeks either side of 07/06/2067) will help Oliver to make pleasant, or beneficial changes at home, making it more idealised, but potentially more attractive, but then again, later on, Oliver may have to guard against any undue enthusiasm there (for 2 weeks either side of 16/11/2067).

Oliver may show an underlying, greater thirst for experience, more robustness and greater courage than normal. Also, he may become more inscrutable, self-sufficient and sceptical (for several years to come). However, in the short term, Oliver's self-assertiveness, and passions, could be stimulated, leading to his usual setbacks. He will be likely to respond more quickly to all forms of excitement, so that self-control may well be needed (for the time between 9 – 12/10/2066). Indeed, for the rest of 2066, Oliver may need to guard against the effects of rashness and of aroused passions. Later, he should make himself as pleasant and as pleasing as possible, because his mind will be peaceful and happy. He could use this time for purifying and refining his personality. This will be a good time for artistic affairs (for 2 weeks either side of 26/07/2067). A further weak, but fortunate influence will cause Oliver's mind to become more hopeful and cheerful (for 2 weeks either side of 20/08/2067). Other favourable influences may be stimulated, while unfavourable ones will be minimised. Some such poor influence may stimulate any latent desires that Oliver may have, into greater activity. Once more, he should guard against rash and hasty conduct, avoid travel when possible, and remain cautious in his dealings. In short, he will need to exercise control, while this 'dangerous' influence lasts (for 2 weeks either side of 26/09/2067).

Mentality: A favourable, but weak influence, will link Oliver's brain with his latent mentality. He could improve his mind by study and reading. He could gain financially by doing this. A busy period is indicated, which may only involve physical agility and quickness, instead of usefully combining these two physical attributes with mental alertness (for 2 weeks either side of 23/02/2067).

Oliver could make a favourable period successful (for 2 weeks either side of 07/08/2067). His active brain and stimulated mental energy will enable him to display as much talent that lies latent within him. By studying, he could learn much under this influence. Good and useful work may be done, not just for the present only, but also for the future. A fortunate influence follows this, and may raise Oliver's consciousness to a higher level (for 2 weeks either side of 17/09/2067). However, even later, an unfavourable influence may cause weird experiences and remarkable dreams. Oliver will become more impressionable and should not go against his common-sense. He has to come to distinguish between the false and the true, and between the real and the unreal (for 2 weeks either side of 24/10/2067).

Oliver's attention may be turned towards things psychic, or occult. Science or philosophy may be studied and the deeper side of religion investigated (for between 5 to 7 years in total). A favourable, concurrent influence for Oliver's mind would bring aspiration, clear thinking, intuitions and philosophic thoughts (but for one year only). He may be able to make much progress in developing his spiritual insight (between 20/09/2066 and 26/02/2067).

Lifestyle: Following a decade of desire for intellectual advancement and mental improvement, which will have brought Oliver an enhanced sense of refinement and accession of thoughtfulness, he will now begin a more peaceful and evenly balanced decade containing more pleasure (and quiet) than formerly. Someone might enter his life, so that their two careers can run on similar lines, and each will be working in the same groove. Much of Oliver's responsibility of life will be shared and thus his pathway will become soothed. This will be a marked feature of this period. A stage has been reached when the active bustle and turmoil of life, will be put to one side for a time. He may cultivate an improved vision, in which the subjective will become clearer, and comparisons more appreciated. There will be an 'internal' progress that will manifest later.

Oliver could have made much of an ending period (lasting for 3 years but ending at 11/2066) financially, socially and affectionately. There could have been advancement, recognition and a general uplifting during this time. Now there will be an opportunity for starting a fresh phase of experience (lasting for some 3 years). Oliver's power of self-assertion, to show and gain recognition for his abilities, will be stimulated. He could become imbued with a singleness of purpose, but it will be essential that he direct his aspirations only towards worthy goals. At this time, he should send his thoughts outwards, as well as to seek to help others as much as possible. A further good influence (lasting for 3 years) will favour his health, vitality and bodily energy, so that he will be able to cope better with business, profession, or otherwise. As a result, there may be promotion, public recognition, honour or fame.

Occult affairs may become more prominent in Oliver's life (until about 08/2068).

Relationships

Others: Quarrels are possible for the short period between the 11-14/10/2066 with more, possibly coupled with much opposition, for the following two months. During this mildly unfavourable influence (for 9 months either side of 10/2066) it would be better if Oliver could avoid dealings with anyone who was not favourably disposed towards him, thereby preventing delay and worry. Also, he will need to be careful when communicating with others to minimise indiscretion in both speech and writing. Oliver might act too forcefully without due regard for the rights and feelings of others (a poor influence, but weakening slowly over the next 18 months).

But Oliver will have become more popular with the elderly, with the responsible, and within his own sphere of responsibility (for 2 weeks either side of 30/03/2067). Additionally, there is a favourable influence for all pleasures, etc. (for 2 weeks either side of 26/07/2067).

Oliver may become over-anxious and brooding. It could be a bad time for engagements, dealings and new undertakings. His best course would be to cultivate as much hope and cheerfulness as possible (for 2 weeks either side of 07/09/2067). Also, an unfavourable influence warns Oliver to be very careful in his dealings with others. He may experience fraud and deception (for 2 weeks either side of 24/10/2067).

Friends: A cheerful and adaptable attitude may help Oliver to form new friendships (from 07/2067 to 05/2071). There are likely to be social gatherings of a more-or-less 'bohemian' character (from 08/2065 to 05/2068). Oliver may make radical changes, resulting in fresh contacts, at this time (for 2 weeks either side of 04/11/2066). Possibly, new friends will be formed (for 2 weeks either side of 11/08/2067) but also, Oliver should guard against undue generosity, or the making of new friendships (for 2 weeks either side of 16/11/2067).

Family: Oliver's father may suffer (from 11/10/2066 to 14/10/2066) and there may be domestic problems (for 4 months from 10/2066). Oliver will need to show prudence in all his dealings with servants and elderly relatives (for 2 years after 10/2066). There may also be some trouble involving his mother, or wife (for 2 weeks either side of 27/11/2067). Deaths may occur within Oliver's family circle, or death may affect him in some way (for about 2 years from now until 07/2068).

Lover: The time (for 2 weeks either side of 24/01/2067) may not be good for dealings with members of the opposite sex. Also, his lower nature can become excited, making it difficult to manage, but only because of the increased force operating (for 2 weeks either side of 07/06/2067). Many quarrels and much opposition may occur within Oliver's marriage (for 4 months from 10/2066). There may be a loss of income concerning his partner's money (for 2 years until about 07/2068).

Career

Early: (For 15 months either side of 10/2066) financial affairs will be brought to the fore. Oliver should be able to take advantage of this to increase his income, either through investment, or by engaging his mind generally with finance, for his own benefit. Concurrently, there is a weak, long-lasting, but diminishing, unfavourable influence making Oliver's mind over-active and so inclined to become hasty and too easily excited. Oliver should be careful in all his dealings, guarding against fraud particularly (from 07/2065 – 07/2066). A weak, but possibly fortunate influence, suggests beneficial changes in occupation. Some new pursuit may be started, and public dealings, or with the many, could go well (for 2 weeks either side of 05/12/2066, and similarly for 30/12/2066). However, Oliver may suffer trouble in his occupation through persons in authority (from 06/08/2066 – 08/12/2066). In fact, briefly, there may be trouble at work through superiors (from 11-14/10/2066). Alternatively, Oliver may enhance his popularity by his ability to arouse mass emotions (for 2 weeks either side of 04/11/2066).

Financial matters may continue to need attention, because a wasteful, expensive time could lead to anxiety (for 2 weeks either side of 24/01/2067). This could cause Oliver to exercise more thought, prudence and management of his own affairs (for 2 weeks either side of 30/03/2067). But a malignant spell could cause more trouble and anxiety while it lasts. Oliver may suffer from disappointments, indiscretion and through dealings with superiors (for 2 weeks either side of 19/05/2067). Less noticeably perhaps, Oliver may experience setbacks to his prestige resulting from an inability to work in harmony with others, making for emotional disappointments (from 31/03/2066 – 12/05/2067). An unfortunate and harassing, but weak, influence, and which will depend on Oliver's own attitude towards his surroundings, will incline him to go to extremes concerning waste and extravagance, making him liable to losses (for 2 weeks either side of 07/06/2067). Furthermore, another unfavourable, but weak influence will operate, during which Oliver should try to act from well-defined motives, rather than from impulse and/or personal bias (for 2 weeks either side of 19/07/2067).

However, more favourable changes could be made in occupation and in connection with new undertakings (for 2 weeks either side of 11/08/2067). Improvement for his finances, gain from superiors and in his general surroundings could arise (for 2 weeks either side of 20/08/2067). But later, an unfavourable period for changes, due to compulsion, or restlessness, may lead to setbacks (for 2 weeks either side of 27/08/2067). Moreover, a further influence may not be good for either financial affairs, or for undertaking fresh ventures (for 2 weeks either side of 16/11/2067). Indeed, Oliver's urge to work at the head of a group may arouse popular antipathy thereby causing unfortunate changes, due to his restlessness, or compulsion (for 2 weeks either side of 27/11/2067).

Oliver's ability to draw upon the resources of his group's unconscious may lead him to become compelled to undertake certain work to comply with the needs of the group. Oliver may wish to challenge his established security, and there may be trouble from inferiors. However, foreign affairs, and benefits from abroad, plus extended travel, could all go well.

Vocation: No interpretations were found for inclusion in this section.

Middle: A good influence, lasting for 3 years from now, will favour Oliver's health, so that he can cope better with his business, profession, or otherwise. As a result, there may be promotion, public recognition, honour, or fame. However, Oliver may become liable to financial loss, extravagance and lavishness. Waste may accumulate in his physical system, or in his surroundings. He should avoid litigation, social affairs, or religious matters, due to over-enthusiasm and excess of feeling (from 10/2065 – 07/2068). A weak influence may prove fortunate for coming before the public, dealing with the many, or for making a journey (for 2 weeks either side of 11/08/2067).

Oliver may be able to make significant progress as a result of painstaking and thorough research in some particular field (from 20/09/2066 – 26/02/2067). Oliver may experience a desire to transcend all boundaries through intense emotional experience, but setbacks will be possible through character instability (i.e. too idealistic, or too impractical, or being too sensitive in his constitution) (from

12/11/2066 – 30/01/2067). As we have seen, there may be trouble and upset through financial losses, possibly relating to his partner's money (for 15 months either side of 05/2067).

Charity: A disturbing influence regarding charitable affairs operates (for 2 weeks either side of 07/09/2067) but Oliver should have gained through charitable matters (from 04/2066 – 01/2069) particularly perhaps, through more secluded, or hidden ones (for 2 weeks either side of 11/08/2067).

Late: There were no interpretations for inclusion in this section.

Health

A good influence (lasting 3 years) will favour Oliver's health, vitality and bodily energy. During the short period between 11-14/10/2066, an accident, or feverish ill-health may occur. Also, his health may be affected by feverishness and by impurities in his blood (from 10/2066 weakening to no effect by 04/2068). Inflammatory complaints may also occur (from 12/11/2066 – 30/01/2067). Similarly, his health should be treated with caution (for 2 weeks either side of 19/05/2067). In the background, Oliver's vital conditions might become depressed, causing a liability to chills, for the next two years. But periods favourable for health comprise 2 weeks either side of 05/12/2066 and similarly for 27/08/2067. His health may suffer from inflammatory setbacks (from 12/11/2066 – 30/01/2067). Should Oliver suffer a bereavement (from 01/2067 – 08/2069) then his nervous system may become hypersensitive, perhaps leading to lung trouble. Accidents through fire, electricity and/or explosion could occur between 03/2067 and 09/2070. Excess force operating, may result in accidents, or possible violence (for 2 weeks either side of 07/06/2067). The good condition of his blood may need monitoring (for 2 weeks either side of 07/06/2067) also. In addition, he should avoid any excess of sweet, sugary and sickly foods (from 07/2067 – 05/2071). The periods (for 2 weeks either side of 11/08/2067, and of 27/08/2067) should prove favourable for Oliver's health. Inflammatory complaints may occur (for 2 weeks either side of 26/09/2067) but his blood may need further monitoring (for 2 weeks either side of 10/11/2067).

— —

Interpretations of Secondary Progressions and Transits for the end of Oliver Strate's Third Period, 2094 – 5 A.D. (see pages 179 – 180)

Character

General: There is a good time for all artistic matters (for 2 weeks either side of 06/11/2094. There is also a good time for removals, and changes for the better (for 2 weeks either side of 05/12/2094). These will be important for the future. On the other hand, the time (for 2 weeks either side of 03/02/2095) will be poor for home affairs, removals, or undue enthusiasm, all of which may lead to over-expansive emotion. A favourable influence can strengthen other good influences, such as Moon(p) conjoint Venus(r); or Moon(p) semi-sextile Moon(r); and minimise poor ones, e.g. Sun(p) square Saturn(r); and Venus(p) semi-square Mercury(r); (for 2 weeks either side of 06/12/2094).

A good time for pleasure, social enjoyment and for a possible, sudden, unexpected event (for 3 days centred on 25/01/2095) may occur. But extravagance, vanity, excess of feeling and self-indulgence is also possible (for 6 days centred on 01/02/2095). In addition (for 2 weeks either side of 25/04/2095) changes are liable to end in uncertainty, worry, indecision, loss and disfavour, which could affect Oliver's health, travel and general affairs. A weak influence will not be good for travel (for 2 weeks either side of 08/07/2095). There may be danger from unrestrained feelings, but Oliver could become involved in artistic affairs (for 3 days centred on 12/12/2095). Further, Oliver should keep himself to himself (for 2 weeks either side of 19/12/2095) avoid travel and decline to take-on any fresh undertakings. ·

<u>Mentality:</u> (For 12 months either side of 22/08/2094) a beneficial influence may be hindered, while, at the same time, Oliver's mental vibrations will no longer remain harmonious. He should guard against indiscretion. Oliver may suppress his creative instincts and try to take his pleasures seriously, but may find it difficult to relax (for the next 15 months). But a tendency to over-activity may lead him into carelessness, indiscretion and even into inflammatory conditions (for October and November, 2094 only). A further influence will have activated Oliver's brain (for 2 weeks either side of 01/10/2094) enabling him to show as much talent as he has latent in him. He should be able to make this period fortunate and successful. By study, he would have learned much under this influence and useful work may have been done, not just for the present, but also for the future. Additionally, Oliver's mind will be busy, but critical and irritable as well (around 22/11/2094). Moreover, his consciousness may become raised to a higher level, due to an influence acting (for 2 weeks either side of 05/12/2094). He could become very intuitive and quick to perceive. As a result, he will grow in refinement and originality. To help here, another influence will make Oliver's mind more hopeful and cheerful (for 2 weeks either side of 06/12/2094).

An unfavourable influence can stir into greater activity any latent desires that Oliver may have, thereby causing him to act more from impulse and out-rushing energy, than at any other time. Deliberately, he should guard against any rash, or hasty, conduct (for 2 weeks either side of 07/01/2095). Oliver may experience gullibility, strange experiences and remarkable dreams, as well as becoming more impressionable. Neither must he go against his common-sense, nor fail to distinguish between the false and the real (for 2 weeks either side of 16/01/2095). An influence strengthening Oliver's Mars traits exists (for 3 days, centred on 25/01/2095). There will be a danger of quarrels, impractical ideas, discontent, elusive happiness and discredit (for 10 days either side of 16/03/2095 and of 30/08/2095). There may be reckless, excitable, sceptical, insincere and insolent feelings (for 6 days either side of 12/04/2095). A weak, but poor, influence makes it better for Oliver to avoid disputes and indiscretion, both with inaccurate speech and in writing. He should not sign anything of importance, should keep his own counsel, and trust no-one (for 2 weeks either side of 08/07/2095). Depression, looking on the black side of things and running his vitality down, could affect his health adversely. He should keep himself free from responsibility, and from serious undertakings, by taking things quietly, by trying to maintain contentment and by persevering with a philosophical attitude (for 2 weeks either side of 09/08/2095) [see also a repeat influence, that of 30/08/2095, given earlier for 16/03/2095]. A period of changes, perhaps unfortunate, (for 2 weeks either side of 18/09/2095) may bring varied emotional responses, due to Oliver's own restlessness, or to an element of his own compulsion/obsession. His independence will be intensified (for 3 days centred on 29/09/2095). Also, intensity, and both mental and physical activity will be energised for a short time (around 01/10/2095 and also about 21/10/2095, see below) but he will need to guard against becoming too self-assertive. Alternatively, a favourable influence will bring a sobering and steadying trait into Oliver's life (for 2 weeks either side of 19/10/2095). Some added responsibility may become important while his natural stability is enhanced. He may become more thoughtful and serious than usual, so that his honour and credit will improve. Now would be a good time to arrange his affairs onto a more substantial foundation. Oliver should guard against deception/gullibility, and use his mental energy to push his affairs on (for 3 weeks either side of 21/10/2095). There is danger of imprudent conduct (around 03/12/2095) but his nerves will become quickened making them more alert and sprightly (for 2 weeks either side of 04/12/2095). Also, his magnetic nature will become enhanced, enabling him, again, to respond to a higher state of consciousness. He will become more intuitive, original, ingenious and responsive, regarding all improvements, and particularly those reforms for the good of others.

There will be a poor time (for 2 weeks either side of 19/12/2095) for writing, correspondence and speechmaking. In addition, some unfortunate changes, resulting in uncertainty, worry and loss, will not prove good for his health (e.g. blood disorders) general affairs, pleasure, friends, or attachments (for 16 days either side of 29/12/2095).

<u>Lifestyle:</u> For the next two and a half years Oliver's keen interest in domestic and home affairs will continue. He will have become softer, more receptive and more sensitive, thereby becoming more alive to feelings, sensations and psychic conditions. There may well have been a greater interest in all occult and mystical things. He will have developed a firmer grip on life, and become more persistent, tenacious and keener for more experiences. But shortly after, a critical stage in his development will become reinforced.

During the next decade, there could well be deaths in his family circle, and sorrows through his feelings and emotions. Also, there may be an increased liability to infection, and a tendency to meet with some very disagreeable conditions. Yet he may still develop a far deeper interest in occult matters. Additionally, he may acquire a greater love of secrecy and an acquisition of dignity, but along with some danger of jealousy and pride. Moreover, he may undergo some striking experiences.

(For 12 months either side of 22/04/2094) there will have been an unfavourable period. Oliver may have met with deception, fraud and even treachery. His mind will have become depressed, separation and estrangement may have occurred, and he will have found that those in whom he has placed his trust, may have proved untrue to his interests. Oliver must now become more careful in his dealings with others, and especially he should avoid legal and serious disputes, for all affairs will tend to go wrong while this, and other, adverse influences last.

(For the following 14 months, until the end of 2095) the whole of Oliver's current progressions will tend to become more or less unfortunate. He will/will have met sorrow and grief and there will be a strong possibility that someone in his domestic circle will have passed away. Hence, he will find it difficult to keep his mind free from anxiety and worry, while this influence lasts. He should not make any changes that are not absolutely necessary, and he should be very careful in his dealings with others. If he should allow himself to become too depressed, then this will likely affect his health, such as enhancing rheumatism as a protracted illness. All of this tends to comprise a very trying and unfortunate period, but he should cultivate caution, steadfastness and courage, to come through it.

(For 18 months either side of 10/11/2094) there will be another unpleasant and unfavourable influence operating. There will be drains on Oliver's purse, a tendency to lose money, along with various other disappointments. Existing ties may be severed, he may lose friends, and he may lose those to whom he has become deeply attached. This is a poor time for domestic affairs and his mind will be neither over-cheerful, nor will any pleasurable matters be negotiated successfully.

Oliver's desire for artistic, self-expression may be stimulated (until mid-2096). A young woman, with whom Oliver has a karmic link, may play an important part in his life at this time (which remains until 25/05/2096).

Relationships

Others: There will be danger of quarrels (between 03/10/2094 and 29/10/2094); (between 05/01/2095 and 04/02/2095) and (between 23/06/2095 and 11/07/2095). However, there is a very good influence, denoting a favourable time for all pleasures, attachments, engagements and social affairs (for 2 weeks either side of 06/11/2094). Oliver will respond to all displays of affection readily, and with full sympathy. His mind will now be peaceful and happy. However, there may be some trouble with the aged (for 3 days centred on 17/11/2094). Also (for 3 days centred on 04/12/2094) Oliver's energy will be infused into matters of others, which may require to be met with caution.

A strange and unfavourable influence warns Oliver to be careful in all his dealings with others (for 2 weeks either side of 16/01/2095). Oliver may arouse popular antipathy, due to his own restlessness, or to an element of compulsion. Also, there may be trouble with female relationships (for 2 weeks either side of 11/03/2095). Additionally, there may be difficulties with enemies (for 2 weeks either side of 18/05/2095). Further, a weak influence will only perhaps affect Oliver's feelings, if they have been called-out. Yet there may be benefit, if he can influence others in his favour. Much will depend on Oliver's attitude towards others at this time (for 2 weeks either side of 12/06/2095). But a poor time to deal with others, especially with those who are capable of drawing him out, occurs (for 2 weeks either side of 08/07/2095). (Until the end of August, 2095) Oliver should avoid dealings with those who are not favourably disposed towards him. Analogously, affairs between himself, and those to whom he is attached, may be delayed, hindered, or trying. There may be trouble with women (for 3 days centred on 24/09/2095). An event may isolate Oliver from his fellows (from 16/10/2095 until 10/11/2095). Again, there may be trouble through women (for 3 days centred on 03/12/2095). Once more, Oliver's energy will be infused into matters of others, which will require to be met with caution (for 3 days centred on 04/12/2095). Oliver may suffer from ill-repute, or personal attacks, and should strive to avoid misunderstandings (for 2 weeks either side of 19/12/2095). He should also guard against any unkind thoughts, or wishes, of others (until the end of 2095).

Friends: New friends may be made (for 2 weeks either side of 22/11/2094). Some new friendships, fresh possibilities, or new thought are possible for 2 weeks either side of 05/12/2094). Oliver may find a steady, aged companion (for 15 months until the end of 2095). But a poor period for friends exists (for 16 days either side of 29/12/2095). Additionally, friendships and objectives may cause trouble (from 04/08/2095 until 20/08/2095). He should guard against deception, and he is more likely to suffer than to gain, through friends (for 12 months either side of 10/12/2095).

Family: Oliver will put energy into family matters, which will need to be met with caution (for 3 days centred on 04/12/2094). It may be a good time to visit, even when domestic affairs are going well (for 2 weeks either side of 12/06/2095).

Lover: (For 12 months either side of 10/12/2095) there may be some disappointment regarding an attachment, and adversity regarding the steady flow of affection. In fact, there may be trouble through Oliver's affections (from 15/09/2095 until 02/10/2095).

Career

<u>Early:</u> Oliver's financial affairs will be at the fore. He should be able to take advantage of this to increase his income, either through investment, or through engaging his mind with finance, for his own benefit (for the next 6 months). Pleasant and beneficial changes will occur, possibly in Oliver's occupation, habits, undertakings and pursuits. It is a fortunate time for coming before the public, dealing with the many, or for making a journey (for 2 weeks either side of 22/11/2094) but he will need to guard against quarrelsome subordinates (until 01/12/2094). On the other hand, there tends to be a poor period for either financial, or social, affairs (for 2 weeks either side of 03/02/2095). Extravagance, undue generosity and pushing affairs, should be guarded against. A hasty change of occupation, or a rash enterprise undertaken, (for 10 days either side of 16/03/2095) is possible. Finances may suffer (between 10/08/2095 and 25/08/2095) and (from 15/09/2095 until 02/10/2095) and with authority (from 25/10/2095 until 26/11/2095). But generally, financial prospects will have been enhanced, along with added possessions (until 12/05/2095). There may have been some gain through old established concerns (until the end of 2095). On the other hand, Oliver could use his mental energy to push his affairs, travel and extend operations generally (for 3 weeks either side of 21/10/2095). There is business activity (for 3 days centred on 03/12/2095). Suddenly, Oliver may gain, either by investment, or speculation, or by forming fresh plans, or by joining societies, or through travel (for 2 weeks either side of 04/12/2095). Alternatively, there could be a poor time for financial affairs, for dealing with elders, or authority, and Oliver should now act as discreetly, and as prudently, as he can throughout this time (for 12 months either side of 10/12/2095) because conditions may prove inimical to his material welfare.

<u>Vocation:</u> There were no interpretations found for inclusion in this section.

<u>Middle:</u> Financial considerations will tend to dominate his outlook (for about 20 years). Altruistic ideals will be present but may lack applicability, or suffer from insufficient exertion (for about 10 years).

Oliver may meet strange experiences and may become attracted to the occult (for about 7 years). There is the possibility of gain through several sources, in which Oliver's ability could win high returns.

<u>Charity:</u> For about 4 years Oliver will develop his interest in, and knowledge of, charity, but he needs to guard against clever, tricky and restless subordinates. There may be a good time for charitable affairs (for 2 weeks either side of 28/11/2094) but disputes and misconceptions may arise and interfere with his feeling of equilibrium. Charitable activities may suffer (between 22/07/2095 and 07/08/2095). Oliver will have to guard against disarranging charitable affairs (for 3 weeks either side of 21/10/2095). Energy may be expended on charitable activities, but his ideals may be somewhat impractical (for 3 days centred on 13/12/2095).

<u>Late:</u> There were no interpretations found for inclusion in this section.

Health

Oliver may become sensitive to his environment, e.g. through self-indulgence, contagious diseases, and possible wasting, atrophy and even deformity. He should avoid drugs (for about 10 years). Nervous troubles, such as neuralgia, rashes and peculiar ailments, may occur (for about 7 years). Over-activity may lead to inflammatory conditions (for about 2 months only, i.e. to 01/12/2094)). Excess, or extremes, may make Oliver's blood disordered (for 2 weeks either side of 03/02/2095). Uncertainty, worry, indecision, loss of affection, and disfavour could also adversely affect Oliver's health (for 2 weeks either side of 18/05/2095). Unfortunate emotional experiences may cause him trouble through a sensitive digestive system (for 2 weeks either side of 18/09/2095). A weak influence (for 2 weeks either side of 06/10/2095) may require Oliver to safeguard his health. This influence can become the forerunner of adverse changes in his general well-being. Such troubles may affect his health poorly (from 25/10/2095 until 26/11/2095).

— —

CONCLUSIONS

We have seen that from a person's selected life-events, together with traits from that person's Character Portrait, and along with relevant sections from the Prediction exercise carried out for that time, we judged that the method of Secondary Progressions, coupled with Transits, constituted the method-of-choice for carrying out Prediction exercises. For example, we can now see more clearly the strong, advisory and background role that Queen Mary played for her family, from her Coronation onwards. Similarly, we can see more clearly again, how President Ford coped with the enormous tasks facing him from becoming Vice-President until the end of his Presidency. He had to have relied on his early, various life experiences, and on the advantages shown, at the time, by the sections of his Prediction exercise of Mentality, Friends and his Career under 'Early', as given.

On the basis of these results, we were encouraged to extend these results to cover an example of 'Forwards Astrology' for a boy, Oliver Strate. Now we can't really know what his major life events will be, or when they will occur, but probably, his predictive exercises provided, could be modified rapidly, in attempts to prove helpful at any time in the future, for any decisions needed then.

— — — — — — — — — — — — — — — — — — —

Figure 11: Secondary Progressions and Transits at the end of
Oliver's 3rd Stage, towards the end of 2094, form Epoch.

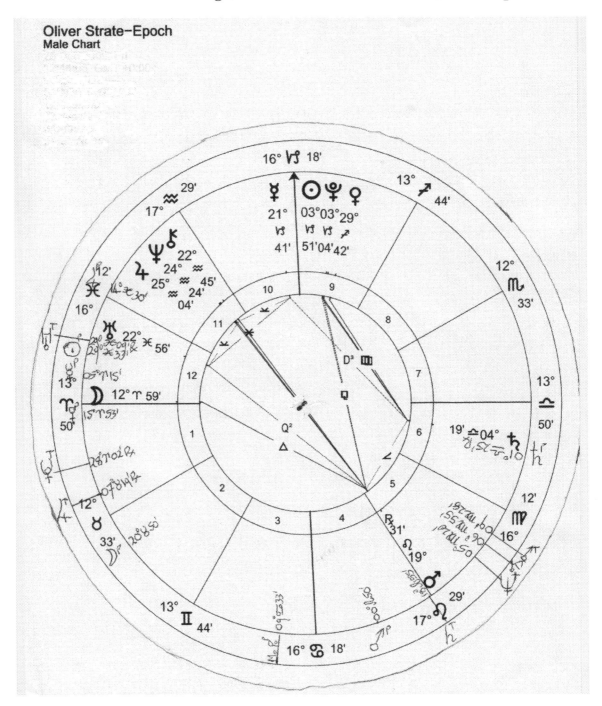

Figure 12: Secondary Progressions and Transits at the end of Oliver's 3rd Stage, towards the end of 2094, from Birth.

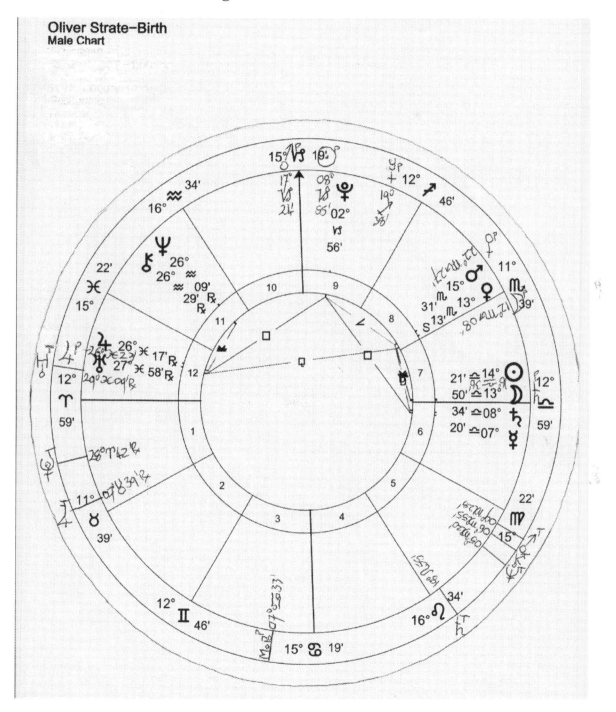

APPENDIX 1

Character Portrait of Mary of Teck – Queen Consort to England's King George V.

I have lost three sons through death, but I have never been privileged to be there to say a last farewell to them."

<u>General:-</u> Mary existed mainly in a World of conflicts, or of definite polarities. Compromise was an essential part of her everyday existence, although she may have felt intimidated by the circumstances that made this necessary. Accordingly, there was an inclination to let matters remain as they were, and to put up with them. Thus, she would have become patiently conditioned to trying circumstances. Generally, her nature was soft, yielding, passive, given to foreboding and so more ready to suffer than to react. There was a tendency to feel timid through feelings of personal inadequacy, as well as towards retirement and philanthropy. However, being independent, her outer behaviour seemed to be based on a belief in the survival of the fittest. She let unpleasantness roll off her back because she didn't take herself too seriously. At the same time, she insisted on her right to assert herself, and she didn't feel that she had to explain her actions to anyone. Her moods depended upon her feelings at any moment. When she was emotionally high, she was outgoing, but she was shaken by any unsettling experience. Because of her emotional nature, she tended to lose her composure under stress. However, she became aggressive only when she had to protect her feelings, and herself, from abuse.

Mary had a strongly artistic personality, with an interest in the psychic, the mystical and the occult. Her energy was expressed forcefully in hard and unstinting work, and she expected the same from others. Although she expressed her energy with strong purpose and creativity, she also expressed it domineeringly with bad temper. However, this also meant that she had stamina for arduous, rough and pioneering conditions, or for the bearing of personal hardships. More quietly, Mary had interesting hobbies and ways of finding enjoyment in life, but with no interest in the hackneyed and the ordinary. She liked life by the sea, was interested in things of the sea, as well as in hidden things, which were pursued with energy and with a desire to experiment in new ways. Her well-balanced inclination would have been towards beauty and ease, but perhaps too irresponsibly and lazily. Although love of peace was suggested, there were tendencies to be showy, extravagant, to squander gains and to trust to luck too easily. Again, although easy-going, affectionate and good-natured, she could also have been uncertain, changeful, inconstant and self-willed. More negatively, on occasion, she could prove to be hasty, headstrong, impulsive, liberal, egotistical, avaricious, harsh and brutal.

Yet Mary was also sympathetic, compassionate, quiet, hospitable and charitable. She received similar considerations from others. She was optimistic, cheerful, and contented with her own surroundings and ways. And so, Mary could have shown a pleasing personality that was refined and enthusiastic for the arts, dancing and music. As a bonus, Mary had a jovial, humorous and witty side, with success through its exercise. She was deserving, mirthful and could have become thoroughly expansive in genial, kindly and emotional ways. She loved company, pleasure and going here and there for visits. Social occasions were much enjoyed. At times, she even realised beneficial influences, which were much admired by those who observed them. Moreover, her vitality was expressed in affairs to do with home, family and basic necessity, all with happiness and self-fulfilment. And yet, concerning essentially everything, duty, conscience and orderliness would have been of importance.

Mentality:- Objective, but mainly subjective, strongly emotional and intuitive, Mary's mind was forceful, incisive, downright and good at debate. It was sudden in action, but full of power and revolutionary content. She was highly intelligent (there were the equivalent of twelve, quintile family aspects in her two charts), talkative, lively and versatile. Quick, and capable of hard, mental work, she had a tendency towards scientific thought, shown by inventive, flashing ideas. Yet charm was added to all her mental activity in an independent and unconventional way. Her ideas and hunches would have come easily, since her imagination was also strong. She desired to achieve good through unusual ways. Her ideals would have been very keen, but her assertiveness would have been softened. There was a tendency towards sweetness of character and behaviour, as well as towards all forms of artistic expression.

She was a mediumistic person, receptive to the requirements of her individuality, but also restless with a great love of change and novelty. She was psychic and fantasy-loving with an intensified sensitivity and an inclination to dip into hidden subjects. Her mind became very receptive to the mysterious and weird. This psychic sensitivity, coupled with any form of idealism, produced good results and high ideals. She would have expressed her imagination strongly (which often came psychically) probably in art. Always she displayed her hospitality, but there was danger of her becoming somewhat superficial. As a result, there was apt to be much dissatisfaction and irritability. She was sometimes diffident, reserved, suspicious and secretive. Whereas she had this good sensitivity, there were inclinations early on, towards day-dreaming, to be impractical and to concentrate on visions of the future, rather than on those of the present. She may have become deluded as to the realities of life, tending to live too much in the clouds, lovely though this may have been. Her imagination could have become confused and gullible so that it would not have been well-directed. Touchiness could have induced escapism, whereupon her mind would have schemed in an involved way. Action would then have come from intuition, rather than from reason. Thus there was the possibility that her vivid imagination, without common-sense, could have resulted in chaos. But to help here, her moods were suddenly changeable enabling her to throw off the static and troubles easily and start new receptive ways and thoughts with good results in the relief of nervous tension.

Yet her mind did work in a detailed, sensible and thoughtful manner. Her curiosity gave her a great desire for knowledge, for intelligent interests and for travel. Her studious, ingenuous, disposition was broadminded, penetrative, prophetic, inspirational and dissimulating. She became uplifted with much seriousness in questions of faith and belief. She knew the importance of thinking for herself, even though she would have been strongly conditioned to pattern her thinking after her parents' beliefs. Actually, she may have come to resent their intrusions. With all of these, long-term results could have been good, if duty had been realised, and appropriate action taken. Caution and limitation would have been expressed as strong reserve and secrecy.

In addition, her mind may not have been so resilient always, and at such times may have turned towards practical and pleasant things. Then communication would have taken place in affairs to do with home, domesticity and in any business to do with collecting. Probably, mental occupations would have been carried out at home.

Lifestyle:- Mary's moods and ways could have been changeable in an acceptable way, since new phases in life were liked. She was often torn between two different emotions. She was kind and just, but tended to encourage the romantic and sentimental side of her nature. She rarely understood herself, or the emotions that played through her from time to time. She was easily psychologised, and suffered from her various moods, being receptive to the mental atmosphere around her. She was inclined to be secretive, and, at times, inspired.

All that Mary tried to acquire kept dissolving. Thus, her financial security was nebulous, as were the values she stood for. Every time that she tried to be firm, she became more pliable. During her early years, she could have been particularly sentimental and even gullible. But as she grew, much of this changed into a truly compassionate and soft nature. Although she would have had much difficulty standing up for what she believed was right, she lived to dissolve any false values within her that she had acquired at any time earlier. She was guided by a high sense of ethics and moral behaviour, for which the public had learned to respect her. She sought truth and wisdom, and strove to improve on the knowledge she had acquired. She was trying to establish a sense of principle, which she hadn't formed thoroughly earlier, and had not truly, up to now, formed in the present, except in areas such as in her career, in her public image and in her sense of duty to society.

Mary's inner reflections about her place in society became her stimulus for the ways she would have liked to transform it. She spent much time reviewing the prestige and dignity that she had attained in the past. Through this, she determined her present opinion of herself. As such, she was status conscious, particularly in her peer group. Unusually, she was judging herself in terms of past peer groups, and of how she measured up to, or surpassed them, now.

Work was done to achieve high ideals, even though they may have been visionary and unattainable. Mary experienced the meaning of life at its most basic level. She had very deep insight, most of which came from her own personal experiences. Constantly living on the point of destroying herself, she kept throwing away all that she had gained, because of the lack of deep meaning that she saw ultimately in almost everything. She believed that behind all that which she could perceive at that moment, was the reality that she knew existed. The building of her substance took place in her sub-conscious, and the momentary fascinations of life, did not fulfil her in the least. She was always of an inner, heavenly reality, which kept drawing her towards its centre. She could have become a crusader, trying to transform the society she lived in, as (i) a rebel against orthodox tradition, or as (ii) a seeker of truth wishing to transform humanity, or as (iii) an improver wishing to transform herself.

Mary tried to balance life emphases at contrasting points in her experience. There was a persistent move to a balance, which produced a characteristic rhythm, and which could have been expressed, over-literally, in the figure of a teeter-totter. At all times, there was a tendency to act under a consideration of opposing views, or to a sensitiveness to contrasting and antagonistic possibilities. Rebellious when she wanted to assert herself, she was sometimes indiscreet. Her unique code of ethics was framed in universal concepts, rather than in terms of society's guidelines. But she often moralised on other people's social behaviour.

Mary would have dipped deeply into life, and would have poured forth the contents of her experiences with unremitting zeal. Because her inner and outer Worlds were quite different, she may have had difficulty in making a fulfilling life for herself. The tendency was that she had strong family ties, and even if she had moved away from her home, say in London, she would have returned there often to renew old ties.

Relationships

Others:- Generally, Mary was easy to get along with, and she tried to cultivate the most favourable relations with everyone in her immediate environment. There was ease in attracting others, or the public in general, by sheer, innate charm. She rarely made promises that she didn't keep, so that people would have respected, or admired, her. People were almost always very interested in what she had to say, whether as individuals, or as the general public. People needed her as much as she needed them because she was able to appraise their problems objectively, and find solutions. An important feature of her life was getting involved in circumstances relating to others' needs, either publicly, or privately. At her best, she would have been a great instructor and inspirer of others. Mary's desire would have been to work for the care of others. She became happy with the role of hostess. She felt that it was especially important to avoid conflict at all costs, because she became so disorientated by a lack of harmony. Unfortunately, Mary could be explosive, which was likely to end conditions, and force new beginnings, with unhappy actions and results. Also, she had a tendency to advance herself through ruthless behaviour towards others. Thus, at her very worst, she could have become an agitator, or a malcontent. Fortunately, there was communication in affairs to do with partnership of any kind, or in any matter, which implied reciprocity, or rapport, with others. While it annoyed her to have to concede to people when they were wrong, yet she feared alienating them, if she didn't. On the other hand, she hadn't to listen to people who said, "You can't do that", or, "You can't do this". Also, she hadn't to deny herself something because others had made her feel obliged to them. This would have been slavery, not loyalty. More positively, philosophical arguments would have given her a welcome opportunity to challenge others in mind-to-mind combat. However, as soon as she had become firmly established, she went back to being honest with herself, and with others.

In Mary's outer World, she became very fixed in her attitudes, and there were few who could have swayed her from whatever purpose she felt that she had. She could have got away with doing things that others would have been criticised severely for, but sometimes she took chances that she regretted later. In fact, she took enormous chances that she wouldn't encounter someone, who would have resisted her more strongly than she had bargained for. Some people would not have let her have her own way.

Friends:- Mary often made new friends. Her friendliness was endearing to others. Mary was a friend to all, and rarely too busy to listen when someone needed her, especially when it concerned their future goals and aspirations. By way of return, friends may have offered her needed opportunities for success in her career. Through her friends she could have learned to become more self-confident in social situations. However, she tended to become suspicious of her friends, assuming that they wanted her friendship only because she was willing to do favours for them. Thus, there was loss of friendships and disappointments.

Family:- There may have been a cleavage in Mary's life relating to her parents, or to early childhood. The resulting disharmony in her nature may have urged her to accomplishment. Her relationships with brothers and sisters would have been happy, and they were likely to have been good-looking and attractive. Her family ties may have become so strong that they deprived her of a life of her own. Too much loyalty to family concerns may have resulted in some alienation and guilt. Only when she would have become sure enough of her talents, could she have dismissed anyone, including a member of her family, who had said that she, "couldn't do this", or, "do that". Mary could have so easily become annoyed, when her parents tried to interfere with her goals.

Mary's desire would have been to collect, and to maintain, family and home. Satisfying the needs of the people she loved, may have given her enough reason to achieve. Her energy was expressed in gay enjoyment of children. She might have indulged her own children, just to, "get them out of her hair", but she may have regretted this later, when she had been faced with the effects of her insufficient discipline. But usually, she included her children in her plans, and as they grew up, they would have had fond memories of their formative years. She kept the lines of communication open, so that they could always have shared with her their fortunate experiences, as well as their problems. They knew that she would have helped them with their burdens. Thus, Mary would have offered her children opportunities to grow, and to reach, their full potential. Mary had unusual children, but often there was separation from them.

<u>Lover:-</u> Improving Mary's self-image would have helped her to cope with her personal relationships. Her sparkling conversation attracted romantic partners. Love affairs would have been numerous and happy. Her energy was expressed in gay enjoyment of love-making. The tendency was that unusualness in her expression of love, or in artistic accomplishment, or in any kind of partnership, was delightful and fascinating. Her attachments were unconventional, and with little regard for convention. She had a strong desire nature and wouldn't have accepted "no" for an answer. But taking responsibility in a romantic relationship could have proved painful for her, and she wouldn't have wanted to make a permanent tie. She didn't seek out binding relationships because she felt that they restricted her freedom. There was an easy slipping away from one attraction and the quick forming of another. Parting was likely but for good reasons, and with pleasant replacements, or reunions. But partnerships were very important to her, and if her partner hadn't co-operated with her, then she easily forgot that he had ever existed. In choosing an associate, friend, or lover, she was selective, preferring someone who was mature, and willing to make a substantial contribution to their relationship, so that it would have endured. Partnerships may not have been what they seemed, with conditions kept hidden. Love tended to be intense, sexual, secretive and passionate. And so, her deepest emotions became very one-pointed.

Mary would have been slow to make a partnership, but reliable once settled. She would have been steadfast in love, but possessive. The tendency was that duty, or some form of limitation would have stopped her full expression of love and harmony, but the duty appeared to have been accepted, or less heavy, because of some happiness that it brought. Mary may have married early, to escape from conditions at home, but provided that her identity remained intact, then there was no reason why it couldn't have become a happy marriage. If her parents hadn't approved of the partner she'd chosen, then she may have had to make a painful choice. She could have experienced deep anxiety about this, but making a life for herself depended on it. Her mate would have had to accept her for what she was, because it was nearly impossible for her to change. Also, her partner must have been a friend and have given her the freedom to serve others in her own way. Neglecting her moral responsibilities could have destroyed everything she had gained. She hadn't to have assumed that people wouldn't have known the difference, because they would, although they may not have reacted immediately. She may have married a foreigner, or have lived abroad after marriage, but disappointment was likely with these. Possibly, her partner would have been older, or that her marriage had been delayed.

Career

Early:- Although it seemed that Mary's fate was rarely under her control, i.e. some compelling force behind her appeared to push her on towards good or ill unconsciously, nevertheless, ultimately her destiny lay mainly in her own hands, as well as in the hands of others, to some extent. There would have been opportunities for her alone, and good luck together with a tendency to a fortunate journey through life; all of which would have been expected. She was fond of fame, and enjoyed public recognition. She enjoyed sensationalism and would never have needed an agent to promote her assets. Her activities were both eventful and changeful.

Mary had strong religious beliefs, which were the reason behind her deep, spiritual need to help people through her own creativity. She sought fulfilment and may have craved for adventure. She was optimistic about her ability to succeed but tended to take-on more than she could handle. She was generous to a fault, so that she didn't get the full benefit from her efforts.

Whereas Mary did everything enthusiastically, she sometimes lacked the self-discipline required to get the most from her efforts. Her impatience made her less efficient, but her aggressiveness became useful when the time came for action. Thus, she did have the courage and daring to take advantage of her creativity. Satisfying her ambitions would have been important for her. She was motivated by self-interest and never missed a chance to show her abilities. But her main limitation was apathy. She became easily distracted by romantic affairs and by other pleasurable activities. When her plans went awry, she may have made excuses, because it was painful to realise that she had made a foolish mistake. It became important that she learned to postpone any action until she was sure that her plans were valid. The main obstacle keeping her from exercising her creative options, was a lack of money. This lack of money would have taken the wind out of her sails, until she had learned to conserve her resources. She would have found it painful to restrain her indulgences, but she had no other choice.

Mary had great creativity, and a flair for finding ways to exploit her talents. She realised that she had unusual creative gifts, but she may have put-off using them until she had found a suitable vehicle that would have dramatized them and herself. Effort was made to attain her ideals in unusual ways. But she could have gained an even greater advantage over her opponents, if she had developed her mental assets. She would have claimed little credit for her talent, unless she had taken responsibility for developing it. It became essential that she improved her self-image, which she did by getting a formal education. Generally, seriousness and concentration gave good results with studies. This would have allowed her to compete successfully. She would have become able to deal effectively with the problems of the real World, and not have allowed abrasive situations to disturb her emotionally. She needed to develop her creative imagination in order to become productive. She had had to raise her credibility by capitalising on her gifts. There was a tendency for her, for a willing acceptance of duty, and success through orderly and practical ways, but possibly a personal limitation caused her some lack of gaiety. Yet education would have helped her to find a way to express her understanding, compassion and concern for less fortunate people than herself.

Mary could have progressed more rapidly, and have become more self-reliant, if she had lived apart from her family. It wouldn't have been easy for her to gain the career position she wanted, because she wasn't really sure that she could have achieved this on her own.

Also, breaking ties with the past was difficult, but necessary, if she was to become self-sufficient. She had to have been willing to pursue her objectives alone. If she had wanted to be free from obligations to others, then she had to have made plans for her own future. If she had diversified her skills, then she would always have had a job, and nothing then would have been left to chance. In addition, family responsibilities may have interfered with her freedom to choose a life of her own. She might have met problems, if her parents had disapproved of her goals. Moreover, there was a tendency that she could have become independent and secure only by accepting her responsibilities. But unless she had insisted on greater self-determination, it would have become difficult, later on, for her to meet the demands of a career, as well as of her relationships. Furthermore, avoiding public exposure would have denied her the opportunity to exploit her skills and acquire self-reliance. When she was on her own, she would have learned to assert herself, to have accepted the occasional setback and to have taken on the challenge of competition. She had to have experienced the joy of being truly independent, and have realised that she was competent to make the most of her mental assets and resources.

Mary's need for communication, would have brought her into close, personal contact with the public. The resulting exchange of ideas would have been mutually beneficial, for her greatest opportunities would have come through such contacts. Indeed she was qualified to help people with their problems because she understood their needs. She communicated effectively that she could have handled their needs and they would have been impressed when she had lived up to her promises. The public became confident that she would always have given them full value. People knew that she could be trusted to handle their affairs and provide them with services. It became critical for her continuing development that she helped others to become self-sufficient. In a sense, she owed that kind of effort to society because she was so intimately aware of what was needed. But she also had to cope with her own feeling of insufficiency, and it would have taken her considerable effort to satisfy both the demands of others made on her, while simultaneously fulfilling her own needs. Until she had felt secure, she would have focused primarily on her own interests.

But as she matured, and realised that doing for others could have been fascinating and rewarding, she would have given them the attention that they needed. If her efforts had been appreciated, then it meant that she had developed worthwhile skills, and would have been making a worthwhile contribution to the World. She had always known that the public would have bought her services when she had had the time to develop her ideas and to make them work. Her self-doubt about her abilities would have faded as she grew increasingly successful in meeting the challenge of competition. Working with other people was suitable for her temperament and her colleagues would have been better off too, because of her efforts on their behalf.

Mary tended to become a specialist rather than a jack-of-all-trades. Indeed, because she wanted to be the very best in what she did, she may have had to specialise. She needed to learn a skill and become so competent in it that she would never have had to fear the challenge of competition. She sought a profession that offered her opportunities for continual growth. She knew that she would had to have grown and developed in order to have lived up to her potential. She had to have started at the bottom, if necessary, and then have re-educated herself as opportunities came along, so that she would have been ready when a promotion was offered. She should have learned to like herself for her achievements.

Vocation:- Mary had a special capacity, or a gift, for some particularly effective kind of activity. She had a characteristic and important direction of interest as well as a particular and rather uncompromising direction to her life effort. If she had believed in herself, then she could have achieved almost anything. Capitalising on her creative imagination, but being realistic about her abilities, would have prevented disappointment. She could have succeeded in a career serving the public, and enjoyed a comfortable income without anxiety about material security. She might have chosen a career in which she became a catalyst for people who were unaware of their talents. She may have considered becoming a vocational counsellor, even though, at times, she needed advice herself. She would have been a very good servant, subordinate or employee; very correct in details, although sometimes lazy. Medicine, nursing (eccentricity was shown in taking care of anyone, or anything), financial investment, counselling, insurance and retirement programs, constituted some of the many careers that would have been suitable for her.

There was some likelihood of travelling, but with frustration of plans when travel had been arranged, difficulties abroad, or with foreigners, or with journeys undertaken for dutiful reasons. She may have gone into partnership abroad for business, or profession. However her contact with foreigners would have been better, if they had been elderly.

Also, there would have been success in writing strange and outré novels, and in uncommon pursuits. There was success on water, and dealing in liquids, in shipping enterprises, hospitals, asylums, hotels and in places where the public are catered for, as regards their physical well-being. Her charity would have been expressed flexibly.

Middle:- Unless Mary had believed in herself, she couldn't have realised her dreams. She didn't make exaggerated claims about herself and she had to have learned how to get the attention of people, who could have opened doors. Also, she wasn't always sure that she could have carried out all her plans because she doubted her ability to live up to the enormous responsibility of success. Yet she mustn't have underestimated what her talent could have accomplished when used imaginatively. Her sheer, dramatic, scintillating, bigness of personality, and belief in herself, could have led to outstanding results.

Mary dedicated herself to her position. She felt a strong sense of responsibility and had to have accounted to herself for everything she did. She was deeply concerned with seeing her life as some sensible, formative structure, which had followed a more, or less, reasonable track from the beginning of her memory to the present moment. She tended to be rather crystallised in this respect, to the extent that reason and logic may have eluded her. If something meant deviating from her pre-programmed sense of duty to her self-image, then the only way that she could have been swayed, was if it had included the possibility of her improving her self-image, as long as nothing in her past was destroyed in the process. Great things could have been achieved, if she had worked hard in her expansive periods and had used every opportunity that had arisen. Conversely, she had to have taken a long-view, and have tried to remain cheerful and optimistic, during depressive times. She may have become interested in a cause, but with much less concern over end results, and with no basic desire to conserve either herself, or her resources. She would have been far more apt to adapt her allegiances to lines along which she could have made her efforts count for the most. With her deep, satirical skills, she could have seen to the bottom of problems; to the deep compulsions under which everyone lives. She had an affinity for solving problems that required sophisticated solutions.

Mary's combination of intuition and will-power could have produced unusual results in unusual ways. Very hard work may have been done for idealistic ends. Results may have been disappointing and elusive because all was too imaginary. Over-imagination without common-sense could have produced chaos. Irregular, over-glamorous, escapist ways may have brought downfall. On the other hand, imagination and psychism could have been brought to concrete use, and for money-making purposes. There was a tendency to leadership and success. She had enormous creative resources that she could have harnessed for her own benefit. Her need to be free and secure inspired her to capitalise on her ideas. She was clever at devising money-making schemes, for she understood how money talked, and she used this knowledge to further her ambitions. Because her ideals and imaginative intuitions were kept in bounds, and given shape and form, they would have helped her excellent, strong character-traits to succeed in this material World. However, limitation was felt through difficulties, which could have been hard to grasp, or to have come to terms with, and so may have had to be kept hidden. The tendency was that schemes came to frustration, due to impracticality. Also, there was a tendency for an undermining of control, and of purpose. She came to feel that her efforts had failed to produce the wanted results, and assumed that she had over-estimated her abilities. But she hadn't to have criticised herself too severely, when her earnings decreased, because the fault may have been more general, and have not been connected with her own ability.

Mary preferred to abide by the rules because of the losses that could have resulted, if she hadn't. Also, she was willing to go on without some of life's pleasures temporarily, in order to guarantee her future security. Although vague about money matters (and she may easily have lost her possessions) she would have been idealistic about them. She had a deep respect for material possessions as symbols of her accomplishments, as well as of extensions of herself. There was trouble with finances and monetary difficulties but because she also had the power to make money there was financial success through increased turnover. Once she had understood that achieving depended on being competent, she ought to have considered getting more training through formal education. In this way, her resourcefulness in capitalising on her basic skills, would have allowed her to earn a comfortable income. She didn't hesitate when there were material benefits to be gained, and she was determined to promote all her own ideas for her own advantage. But she had to have kept herself informed about business trends and have got whatever training was necessary to remain efficient. She hadn't have failed to do this because that would have enabled her to demand as much for her efforts as the market would have tolerated. Possibly, she felt that she wasn't earning enough for her efforts, and came to realise that the best way to take full advantage of her creativity would have been through formal education. All told, by paying attention to reality she could have risen to considerable prominence.

Mary's force and initiative were canalised, while her caution and patience were enlivened. There was a tendency that her constructiveness could have forced to a patient working out of what had been started, but not with ease. Also, her results had to have been battled for. Thus, she achieved through painstaking effort. Additionally, these tendencies could have produced selfishness, narrowness and egocentricity. As a result, hardness would have been endured, and sternness given.

Mary's intellect was profound, but she still considered it necessary to test public opinion before taking any action that might have reflected badly on her credibility. She went to great lengths to gain acceptance in a social environment that would have improved her social standing. She may even have indulged in social politics, if that would have enhanced her social position. Usually, she knew what people expected of her, and she was willing to go along with them, knowing that this investment of time and effort would have proved beneficial in the long run. Always the entrepreneur, she sought out important people continually, who could have introduced her to a wide circle of social contacts. She regarded this, too, as a worthwhile investment, despite the personal sacrifice involved. But her rise to public prominence would have been easier, if she had understood just how much she would have needed to know, to win people's respect.

Mary knew the value of arts, and probably she had a good sense of appreciation of music, but she didn't feel that she should have pursued these, as much as she would have liked to. The drive nature for her to seek these had to have come from elsewhere in her nature, which it did.

Charity:- Personally, Mary was mildly interested in philanthropy. However, her love of people, and her high ideals, gave her a responsibility to use her creativity for the benefit of others. Although she had fairly good judgement in handling relationships, she actually hated to make hasty decisions regarding charity. She needed to appreciate, and learn from, others' opinions, to decide where her greatest charitable opportunities lay. She needed to concentrate more on her charitable goals and objectives. Education regarding charity became essential for it gave her the ability to understand the people with whom she would become involved. She developed many charitable ideas for gaining a good situation. Travelling for charity would have been enjoyed. Her charity benefitted through her charm of speech and pleasantness of manner, while not forgetting that it also derived from the exercise of a cheerful, humorous and witty mentality. Ease rather than strength would have been gained. Thus, her charity was expressed with versatility, combined with constructiveness in the use of her mind when speaking about charitable inclinations. But her charity could also have been forceful, incisive and quick, or sudden. The unusual was preferred concerning charity, which would have been conducted in an independent and unconventional way. There was a tendency for her to plan a program for security, containing responsible charity, during her later years.

<u>Late:-</u> Mary dreamed that in her later years, she would have been free to indulge in all the activities she had postponed. She was gifted with ideas that she could have cultivated for future enrichment. Planning would have been a high priority for her. She dwelt in the future and worried about whether or not she would have been financially and emotionally secure in her later years. She should have started to think about becoming independent, so that she could have sustained herself in her later years, and so have reached the goals that she had chosen. She looked forward to the time when she could have been free of the daily harassment and effort of earning a living. If she had used all her resources and talents, then certainly she could have reached that goal. She should have conserved her tangible assets and have established a retirement program that she could have adhered to without difficulty. She had to have tried to accept reality, and to have learned how to use her creative imagination to build-up her tangible assets for her later years. Instead of feeling sorry for herself, she had to have uncovered her hidden talents, and have put them to use.

Appearance and Health

<u>Appearance:-</u> Mary would have been of middle stature, physically strong and moderately good-looking, with a stout build later. Her face and person may have been fleshy with a tendency towards a double chin. She would have had full, soft and mild eyes, plentiful dark hair, together with a pale, soft complexion, strongly opalescent, with a mother-of-pearl tint and lustre. Her limbs may have been small and short. Her bodily communication, i.e. walking, motoring, etc., would have been undertaken keenly and with speed. By contrast, her speech, thought, gesture and movement could have been slow and smooth. She may have had a good singing voice. She would have had a vital, studious and ingenuous disposition, loving music, art, mirth, company and pleasure. Overall, a somewhat Johnsonian character.

<u>Health:-</u> Mary had good health and strength both physically and emotionally. Yet her health was not particularly favoured regarding a liability to feverish complaints, physical overstrain, a lack of self-reliance and a tendency to falling. However, she was nutritive. Also, nerve tension resulted in irritability and disruptive behaviour.

Tension could have snapped, causing tragedy, but relief would have been found by removing herself from company for a while, and by doing what appealed to her most. Additionally, strong fears may have played upon her nerves, undermining her health, along with a possible susceptibility to fish poisoning and to harm from impure water. Her liver may have been affected. Also, there was a liability to suffer from gout, impure blood and boils. In addition, there may have been ailments arising from cold, or damp feet. There may have been a liability to bunions, dropsy complaints and chronic irregularities in her system, together with the possibility of unusual diseases.

— — — — — — — — — — — — — — — — — —

Figure 1:- Epoch Chart for Queen Mary of Teck.

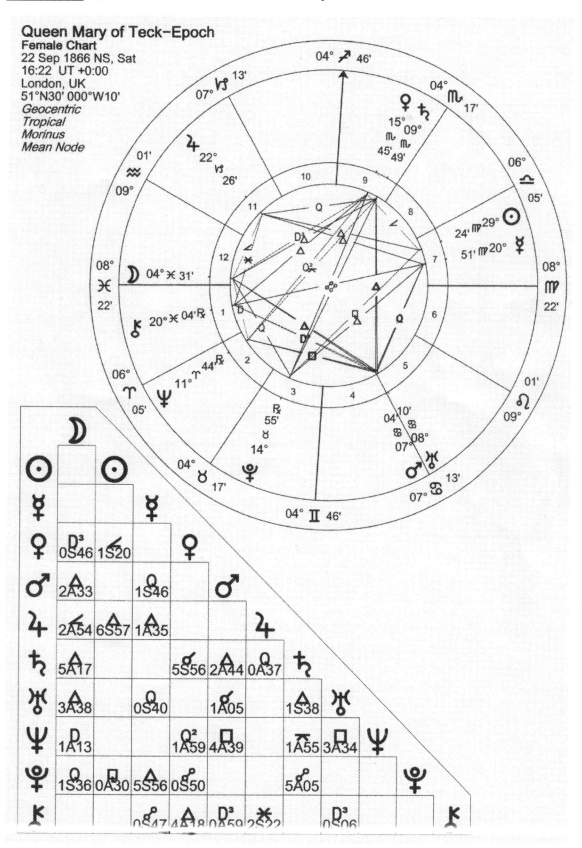

Figure 2:- Birth Chart for Queen Mary of Teck.

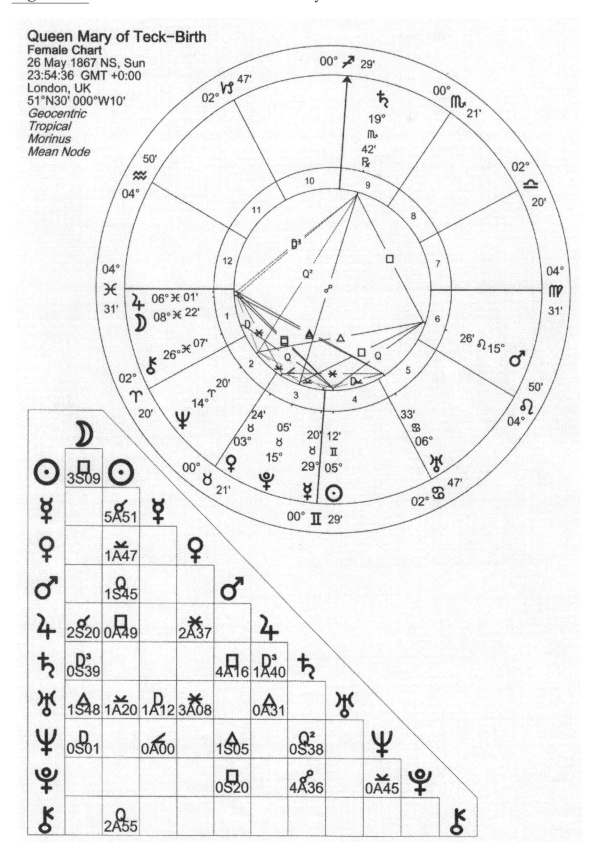

APPENDIX 2

Character Portrait for The 38th President of the United States of America: Gerald R. Ford.

"Our Constitution works. Our great republic is a government of laws, and not of men. Here the people rule."
From the President's swearing–in address.

Character

<u>General:</u> Gerald's personality would have been far too active for his individuality, but his emotional and devotional nature would have been stimulated, giving him much activity with speech, restlessness and a yearning for the unattainable. His power and vitality were expressed intensely, passionately, secretively and penetratingly, in secluded, or hidden, ways. Also, he would have had psychic gifts, inspirational speaking, an ability to prophesy, or to bring dreams through into his brain. He had a changeful, companionable and kind nature. In addition, he showed ambition, dignity and self-reliance, as well as careful, plodding activity. His manner appeared to be cool and cautious, and he seemed more limited than he was really. Duty, conscience and orderliness were of importance. He was inclined to be timid through a feeling of personal inadequacy. There was an adjustment to conditions, and an attempt to by-pass difficulties, but with nervous stress. But also, there was a tendency for him to free himself from bounds and ties. Usually, he didn't seek the limelight of public recognition, but he accepted it humbly, knowing that by doing so, he would only have been doing what anyone else would have done in his position.

More positively, Gerald's self-expression was shown energetically, being bold, strong, forceful, brave, initiatory, hard-working and quick. He could have accomplished much in a short time. Pleasurable activities would have exerted a great attraction, particularly those involving travel, or the outdoor life. His good disposition was jovial, optimistic, cheerful and contented, as well as humane, social, and courteous. There would have been an intention, also, to surmount his difficulties. He had a good, balanced outlook, a love of beauty, peace, and a lack of worry, in which ease, rather than strength, was gained. As a generous and honourable character, he inspired respect. As a tolerant, kind-hearted, artistic personality, the arts became a necessity of life, bringing happiness and benefit. He was fond of sport, with a great love of horses. Moreover, his power and vitality would have been expressed intuitively, emotionally, guardedly and domestically, particularly in affairs to do with family, home and basic necessities. Happiness and self-fulfilment would have been evident here. Further, he would have had the ability to use the unconscious side of his psyche.

More negatively, as a strong character, Gerald could have been dogmatic, self-righteous, self-assertive, priggish, and full of very keen, likes and dislikes. He could have been showy, exaggerative, conceited, imprudent and extravagant, as well as relying too much on luck. Also, he might have been self-willed, self-insistent, revolutionary, resentful, vengeful and disruptive, as well as awkward, brusque and precipitate with a liability to go to extremes of anger. In marked contrast, his self-expression could have been limited hurtfully, with an inclination to self-pity.

Gerald would have been fond of travelling, exploring new scenes, new ideas, opinions and thoughts, so that success was to have been found in foreign affairs, as well as in religious matters. He liked to move about, and did not like spending too much time in any one place. As such, he was very much the nomad, wandering through life to test the knowledge he had gained earlier, against all current circumstances. Erratic, odd and interesting circumstances would have been met while going about from one place to another. He showed an inclination to all matters connected with the sea.

Mentality: Gerald was mainly subjective but also objective. His mentality was active and sensitive, so that his response was shown in a restless, interesting and cheerful approach to, for example, psychic research and to speculation regarding the after-life. He responded in a desire to work, and to get others to work also. Thought, speech and writing were vivid, unusual, scintillating, inventive, and inclined towards unusual subjects for study. But he may have met trouble through these. His moods were suddenly changeable, resulting in an ability to throw off the static and start new, receptive ways.

Gerald had a vital need for self-expression, but tended to be isolated from other minds. He never failed to state his position to anyone, who would have listened. He took liberties in giving his opinion, even when no-one asked for it. There was a great deal of repetition in his own thought processes. Constantly, he sought to be sure of himself, but the more thoughts he collected, the more he came to doubt what he knew. He complicated his life by collecting too much thought. Interestingly, this doubt was good for him because it made it easier for him to release the thought forms that he had crystallised earlier. In fact, his mission here, was an unlearning process, through which he would reach again, the simplistic state of understanding what he once knew, before he had begun to burden himself with, "the excessive baggage of educated opinions". Then, after going through much worry and confusion, he was able to release all which was of no value.

Gerald's ideas and intuitions tended to be strong through heightened receptivity, but may have been carried out in a somewhat perverse, or cantankerous, manner and with some tension. He had great sensitivity, and potentially good fulfilment of imaginative ideas, but he had to have guarded against escapism, deceit and gullibility. Possibly, there was some conceit connected with his width of mind, rather than with his grasp of detail. There was strength and freedom-loving expansiveness, but with some difficulty of expression. Psychic sensitivity was possible with "Glamour and Clouds of Glory" expected. But generally, his ideas and 'hunches' should have been acted upon. His mind would have suitable for occultism, for working in seclusion and for affairs of the sea. Probably, he would have preferred to study the unusual. Fortunately, in some ways, his mind threw-off worries easily, and began thought anew, but over-violently, explosively and stressfully, so that he was liable to end conditions and force new beginnings, but with unfortunate results.

Gerald was clever, intellectual and curious. He would have been inspired, versatile, always searching and original. He sought to know, to understand and to teach where and when he was asked, but never to impress himself on those who could not have comprehended his innate wisdom. His instinct, subconscious mind, psychic tendencies and social awareness, were all capable of being stimulated. He had a valuable capacity for devising a variety of ways to express himself. Thus, he was even cleverer than he thought, but he needed formal training to direct his mental faculties properly, and so better utilise his ingenuity. His highly developed, psychic ability would have served him well as he sought to fulfil his potential.

Gerald enjoyed the drama of human contact. He believed that he could have learnt more about social relationships by dealing with people, rather than by studying textbooks. His mind and mental outlook tended to be good in so far as charm of speech and pleasantness of manner were concerned. Balance rather than worry was evident. But ease rather than strength had been gained. People were fascinated by his gregarious nature along with his ability to share his ideas. He was authoritative, inventive, could read character and possessed spiritual energy. His intuitions were strong and his desires were towards achieving good through unusual objectives. He was truthful, refined, sincere, impressionable, prophetic and charitable. He had an idealistic personality inclined to intellectual pursuits. He was philosophical, a lover of law and order and more intuitive than imitative.

Gerald's limitation resulted in wise control, caution and common-sense in all matters of correspondence, education and literary work. Also, there was a willing acceptance of responsibility in any such area. Similarly, limitation and control would have affected his mental concepts and expression, so that his thoughts would have been well-considered, deliberate and with a serious outlook. His scope for expression would have become enlarged through his ability in careful, far-seeing ways. His tendency towards prevision was strong, which would have stimulated his idealism.

Mentally, Gerald could have been intense, penetrative and with a depth of feeling, possibly in hurtful ways. At these times, his response would have been quicktempered and unthinking. Wilfulness and insistence on being 'different' would have produced tactlessness and bluntness that would have offended others. His views would have become egocentric and egotistic, so that the ideas and ways of all others would have been scorned, "Everyone was out-of-step, but our Gerald". Additionally, he could have shown a lack of concentration, a desire for freedom at any price, along with a somewhat exaggerated expression of licentious behaviour. Thus, he would have been broadminded, but with some unease of expression. Again, at these times, his mentality would have been over-assertive, rebellious, self-opinionated, precipitate in action, powerful, sensational and revolutionary in intent.

But more quietly, the tendency was that his intangibility could have resulted in vagueness and muddles. He tended to live a little in a dream World, and so make muddles in the real one. He had many ideas, but was inclined to poor fulfilment. He may have been deceitful, but (more likely) have become the object of treachery. He had a tendency to avoid the concrete by day-dreaming, by the effect of alcohol abuse, or by the effect of drugs, i.e. through escapism. At these times, he was likely to have kept his communicativeness hidden, unless otherwise brought out.

<u>Lifestyle:</u> Gerald's generation was marked by a tendency to throw off inhibitions and conventions of earlier times, and to express themselves in more open and candid ways. There would have been a rejection of prudery in speech, especially about sexual matters. Although hurtful to older people, the result would have been a new phase of a more frank and healthy attitude. He would have had a vital search for the meaning of life. Because he was in-tune with the continuing process of evolution in his social environment, he was in the enviable situation of helping to determine the content and quality of society. His psychic awareness of the most pressing human needs forced him to become responsible for making a contribution to improve social conditions. He had the advantage of great, creative potential with which to accomplish this objective. Aggressively, he created constant destruction in old, traditional, habit patterns, so that ultimately, he could have gone through a re-birth, within himself, at the very deepest of levels. He developed in his life a legacy of power

for change, and the more discontented he became with the World around him, the more he began to fathom the mysteries that lay within himself.

Gerald had courage, resolution, resource and independence, so that he was sure to make his mark in life, in some way, for good or evil. He would have become known for his strength of character and will. His struggle would have been for universal harmony. He would have become very practically minded and desirous of bringing all theories to the test of action. In addition, his feelings and intellect might both, or either of them, have become well-developed. He may have lacked coolness, calmness and humility (but see alternative interpretations) in which case he should have pondered the text, "Blessed are the meek, for they shall inherit the Earth. For the race is neither always to the swift, nor the battle to the strong" (which he probably had done).

During his youth, he had often tried to act older than he was. Although he may have been wise, he would not have been heeded until later in life. At the highest level, he could have become very spiritual. He may have had a strong, religious insight, which he had developed. Also, he had the ability to weigh things, so that they were balanced from a centred perspective. In his active life, however, he experienced a very strong stop and go vibration, which did not always allow him to do all the things that he would have liked to do. Often, he paralysed himself by considering things to the point that he was using more scope than actually he needed. In this sense, he could have over-exaggerated the importance of things, by seeing too much of life, as either supporting, or negating, principles that he believed he stood for. He was living through a stage of maturing his understanding of himself, and of the World around him.

His struggle for universal harmony would have involved a balancing of life-emphases at opposing, or contrasting points. It was a persistent move to a balance, which was apt to give a characteristic rhythm, and which could have been expressed in the figure of a teeter-totter. His was not so much an uncertainty of action, but rather of acting at all times under a consideration of opposing views, or through a sensitiveness to contrasting and antagonistic possibilities. Gerald experienced constant conflict between expansion, enthusiasm and optimism with restriction, sobriety and reserve. He had to achieve a balance between these two sets of extremes, before reaching much greater wisdom. Yet he had some difficulty putting what he knew into words. He was able to understand his higher mind, but he did not always believe that he would have been able to communicate that understanding to others. He had a very straight-forward knowledge of God, whereas others, less religiously inclined, would have expressed this through, "How the mechanism of the Universe worked." His greatest growth occurred when he had come to understand that the World around him was very much like the 'Tower of Babel'. People were unable to communicate with each other because they had different conceptual understandings of the simplest words. Thus, the quality of communication with others was always less than he knew it could have been. He sensed the interruption in the steady flow of thought that was caused by language barriers.

Gerald assimilated the needs of his immediate environment and from this he was able to understand how to cope with all that lay around him. He had a tendency to pull away from people because he desired to experience more and more of his natural environment in the place of the sophistication necessary in living up to the social expectations of others. In addition, there remained a tendency for him to be a little bit out-of-time synchronisation, particularly between the future and the past. In blending these two, he had much work to do in gaining a balanced perspective in time. He was enormously inventive, and usually could have displayed rare genius in the understanding of how to do things that no-one else around him could have comprehended. He was learning lessons of self-discipline, so that all of the inner inventiveness that he felt, could have been put to use in the current World that he lived in. He had to have learnt how to be different, without upsetting the structures that he wished to improve later on.

Gerald sought an inner sense of identity, which afforded him a uniqueness of character within the framework of the society, in which he lived. He experienced the conflict of compromising his individuality, in order to keep himself in a position from which he could have expressed it more, later. He may have changed his direction many times, until he had found that special niche, where truly he would have been able to express himself. This would have been good for a career in advertising, and in mass-media communication, through which he could have kept his versatility along with the security that he needed.

Gerald would have been capable of unique achievement through a development of unsuspected relations in life, but he would have been liable also, to waste his energies through his improper alignment with various situations.

Relationships

Others: Gerald would have been conditioned by his early environmental circumstances to feel obligated to the people who had provided him with the necessities of life. He developed a sense of social obligation, and the rewards that others derived from his efforts would have been significant and valuable. His response was shown in the legacies of others, or in contacts with their affairs, e.g. as trustee, etc. He did more for others (including his partner) than he did for himself. They may have even tried to tell him that this was his obligation. However, eventually, he would have learned how resourceful he was, from the people who had benefitted from his efforts.

Gerald was keen to act for the good of others. Little in life went by him, without him studying it clinically. He was constantly questioning the values of others. He was so linked with their values that whether he liked it, or not, he was strongly influenced by public consciousness. He came to feel that he understood why people behaved as they do. Quietly, he worried about others. He was idealistic and imaginative, in a kindly, tender way of protectiveness towards others. In fact, he was inclined to be sentimentally 'woolly' about others. Compassion and sympathy tended to be fine, but he would have been able to accomplish more for them, when he had gained the necessary knowledge and training.

Popularity (and much social life) came from his increased desire to form harmonious relations with others. His biggest lessons centred round the establishment of harmony with them. He knew this, but tended to rebel when the going got tough. Yet he had learnt earlier that his real security had come more from others, than it had from himself. He could have learnt something from everyone he contacted, but instead of trying to match their performances (which probably he'd over-estimated) he should have developed his own talents to the utmost, so that he could have accepted any challenge, and have known that he would have succeeded.

Gerald experienced difficulty in communicating with others. Often he knew what he wanted to say, but not how to say it. He was apprehensive about being accepted by others because he didn't think that he could have lived up to their expectations. Because of his low self-image, he assumed that he was obligated to serve everyone. But if he had developed his creativity, then he could have fitted easily into any social environment because he'd already established his worth to society. He came to believe that he was the guardian of others' thoughts. In dealing with people, usually he knew instantly the point that he was going to make. However, he would have avoided making it until he was sure that the language he used, would have been accepted by other people.

Gerald continued an early lesson in relating to people. Thus, in trying to find the means of gaining the acceptance and approval of those he wanted to please, he collected one crystallised thought form after another. Then later on, his tiniest thoughts carried with them the full weight of all the past thoughts that he had attached these to. And so it became difficult for him to reach the very essence of understanding that he had sought without having to sift through all the gloomy thoughts that he had connected together.

Gerald admired people who could apply themselves to get what they wanted. He helped others when they needed it, but he expected them to have appreciated his efforts for them. He attracted people and encouraged them to be open and frank with him. His winning ways brought him support and enthusiasm for his proposals. But he himself was cautious about revealing all his plans, for fear of losing his advantage over others.

Gerald became impatient with people who just talked about the future. He disliked having anyone question his motives. He gave the impression that nothing really bothered him, but that was not always true. He found it painful to contemplate the possibility that he wouldn't have always been in command of any given situation. But he would have understood his adversaries' limitations and weaknesses. However, his greatest contribution to them, and to himself, would have been to have helped them in their moment of need, thereby earning him their gratitude.

<u>Friends</u>: Gerald was a true friend, just, sincere and fortunate. Often new friends were made. But there was a tendency to frequent breaks with friends, a loss of friendships and disappointments.

<u>Family</u>: There were peculiar conditions associated with Gerald's home. He may have had a 'substitute' home, i.e. an adopted one. His brothers and sisters, or their circumstances, were unusual. Separation from them was likely, but he willingly accepted responsibility for his siblings. He was vitally interested in relatives and neighbours, and idealistic about his home and parents.

Gerald's parents' early training provided the legacy of influence and firm base, from which he achieved independence and security by his own efforts. They considered it important that his future should have been free from anxiety about material needs, and they hoped that he would have appreciated their efforts. He was grateful for their influence, and he knew that his goal-seeking would have fulfilled their dreams. As a result, they allowed him to utilise his creativity in any way that would have given him the most satisfaction and fulfilment. As he grew, he would have learnt how to exploit his potential. Perhaps, he may have been conditioned to repress his creative imagination, preferring to indulge his parents in their desires. He may well have looked for a way to use his talents at home. Clearly, he had strong family ties and even if he had moved away from his birth place, he would have returned often to renew old ties. These strong family ties made it painful for him to detach himself from obligations to his parents. He cared deeply for those who were close to him, and offering them help when they needed it, came naturally to him. As such, his responsibilities to family and to loved ones may have diverted him from his goals temporarily.

Gerald wanted the very best for his children, as well as for his lover, and sometimes he may have been extravagant. He hoped to encourage his children to take advantage of the opportunities he had provided, so that they too, could have reached their goals. He instilled self-reliance in his children, so that they wouldn't have had to depend on him. He was deeply concerned about their future, and he would have felt guilty if he hadn't told them about the hazards that lay ahead. However, he did have high hopes that his children would have risen to important and secure positions. But he hadn't to have devoted so much time to his career that his partner and his children would have been denied the pleasure of his attention, and of his own family's mutual interests.

<u>Lover:</u> Gerald had a compelling need to achieve emotional maturity. His affection was most difficult to express, so that his life tended to be solitary. Any partner brought responsibility. There was a tendency that his affections and partnerships were subject to disclosures, upheavals and new starts, but with trouble and unpleasantness. Thus, there was sorrow and loss through his affections. On the other hand, his unusualness in his expression of love, or in artistic accomplishment, or in any kind of partnership, was delightful, intriguing and fascinating. His expression of love was charming and fluent. He tended to be a romantic at heart, with an ability to cherish, so that he brought much pleasure to those he loved. However, his affection was changeable, and often for more than one at a time. His love affairs were numerous, but he was better in partnership than alone. Hence, he tended to be possessive, stubborn and with a strong affection for those possessed. Also, there was an easy slipping away from one attraction and the quick-forming of another. Partings were likely, but for good reasons, and with pleasant replacements, or reunions. His affection could have been demonstrative and gay, but this became restricted.

Gerald would have been willing to make sacrifices for those he loved, if he had known that they would have reciprocated. He kept his private life separate from his professional affairs, rarely allowing one to interfere with the other. But occasionally, he may have become so preoccupied with satisfying his physical needs that he may have neglected giving his more significant objectives the attention that they needed.

Gerald had a very strong sexual nature. His emotions and desires were deep and very strong. However, his drive was not only physical, but mentally and worldly orientated as well. Whether he expressed it physically, or transferred it to mental regions, this drive was powering all that he sought and understood in the World. To him, sexuality represented one of the deepest mysteries, and one of the most unfathomable questions. He was fascinated that sex motivates some people to do things having nothing to do with sex. His own views on sex were permissive.

Gerald may have preferred freedom to marriage, but then there would have been problems associated with either situation. His marriage should have provided him with comfort and contentment, so that he could have applied himself more completely to the demands of his career. But frustration and disappointment had to have been expected from others in close connection, whether in marriage, or in business. They may have brought much responsibility and losses. But they may also have strengthened him by building up an ability to stand on his own two feet. Alternatively, they may have caused him depression and loneliness through the loss of his partner, or through an inadequacy in forming happy relationships. And so, even though he may have complained often that marriage was boring, he knew that it was a stabilising anchor that kept him from what could have become a lifestyle that was too hectic for him to have experienced and learnt from. He needed to feel protected.

Gerald had been given the opportunity to work-out childhood problems with his dominant parent, by selecting a similar type of wife for his marriage. His passionate nature was very strong, so that there was a liability for him to become rather tyrannical, due to his forcefulness. But he hadn't to try to restrain his mate from becoming more self-reliant, and have not tried to compensate for her unwarranted lethargy. On the other hand, he had to be careful not to become a doormat to his partner's desires. Any relationship required compromises, but this could have deteriorated into an abuse of the privilege. He may have met additional problems, if his partner had resented the time and attention that he gave to his professional interests. He would have had much to learn, if he had allowed himself to experience a process through which he could have become more receptive to ideas that would have seemed beyond his maturity level beforehand. For her part, his wife should have known when to get involved in his pursuits, and when to have let him be by himself. It would have been ideal if she had sympathised with his objectives, and had worked with him to achieve them.

Career

Early: Gerald's destiny lay mainly in his own hands, but also somewhat in the hands of others, and would have depended partly on circumstances. Although a secluded start to life was indicated, there was also a tendency to a hard life overall. There was success in life through merit and personal effort, determination and strength of character, but also possible loss through rash and foolish conduct. There was a strong possibility that success would have been achieved early in life. Energy would have been expressed in financial ways, but also in work for the growing things of the earth. His life would have been fortunate, but not overly so.

There was a tendency to a cleavage in his life, relating to parents, or to early childhood. The resulting disharmony produced in his nature, could have urged him to accomplishment, later. If family obligations had forced him to put off working to achieve his own goals, then he had probably consented to it, even if it had caused him some anxiety and frustration. His parents may have chosen a career for him, but he should have thought for himself, and have found a profession based on his own beliefs and needs. He appreciated the advice he had received in his early years, because he knew that his future security would have derived from it. He had a mind of his own, which would have allowed him to gain plenty of security. But if that family obligation had concerned a family business that his parents had wanted him to take over, then probably, he would have done very well. However and more likely, he had wanted to prove himself by striking out on his own. To achieve the many goals he had in mind, he would have to have made some kind of investment. As painful as it seemed, he absolutely had to get some formal education, or his future would have been limited indeed. He needed to define what he had hoped to gain in life, and the best way to succeed. He underestimated his creative potential, which he had had to develop, so that he would have had the freedom to choose an independent base on which to build continuing fulfilment. He should have realised that getting an education would have been a good start. He was inclined to find out which career would have allowed him to fulfil the most important human needs, and thereby have earned him public approval and respect. Getting an education would have enabled him to define his goals and objectives, and so decide on what training he needed in order to pursue them. He did tend to get the right training, so that he could have provided the needed services, and so would have earned himself a comfortable living. He tended to do his very best when he had got the training he needed to amplify his natural gifts. Without training, his contemporaries might have stolen his ideas and have capitalised on them. He realised that to stay in demand, he must have continued to improve his skills. Learning what the public wanted was his key to finding the best way to apply himself, and he needed constant feedback from satisfied patrons, in order to know that he was making a worthwhile contribution. Generally, he was straightforward in using his resources, and he became annoyed when anyone suggested otherwise. He had to have got advice from sincere and trusted friends, for they were probably more aware of his potential than he was. As an imaginative and creative person, he realised that he couldn't have done everything himself, so he obtained the services he needed from people who were qualified in their fields. He invested his resources as necessary and he expected a favourable return. He had always known that he had the potential for success, and so he spent much time formulating plans for making the most out of his creative ideas. The only problem was whether he was motivated by the financial returns, or again more likely, by the useful service he could have provided to society. Thus, early on, there could have been some internal contest between materialism and religion. Either he could have made the commitment to serve others, or he could have indulged himself by ignoring his spiritual responsibilities to them. Had financial return been his only motive, then he would have been denying himself the truly significant achievements that he could have accomplished.

It would have been important for him to establish his own roots and to have proved to himself that he could achieve on his own. But before he could have taken up any purposeful activity, he must have had a reasonably firm foundation. His childhood environment may have taught him the importance of having his own roots; just like his parents had needed theirs, so that they would have accomplished their objectives. Yet he found this difficult to accomplish because he was never sure that he was doing the right thing. He would have been more successful in his life's endeavours, if he had started from a reasonably stable position, so that his goals would have become more sharply defined. And so, when he had felt secure, then he should have been less apprehensive about doing the right thing in striving to reach his goals.

Gerald was keen to act for the good of others and often in unrecognised ways, so that if his objectives had included serving others, as well as satisfying his personal needs, so much the better. A great test was to have decided which destiny was more important to him, his own, or the one that his parents' had chosen for him. He should have learnt to stand on his own before he could have hoped to achieve any accomplishments. If he had waited for his parents' approval, then he would never have established his own goals. However, with his usual skill, he would have had little trouble convincing them that he would succeed, with or without their approval.

Gerald's depth of study became confused, because his ideas had not been sufficiently concrete. Even though it took a lot of hard work to succeed, it would have been easier if he had become well-informed and trained. Self-analysis would have helped him to appraise his potential more positively. In time, he would have concluded that he was far more qualified to succeed than he had realised previously. But at other times, he had tended to stand in his own light, and had met suffering through self-inflicted sorrows. With proper training to improve his sense of self-worth, he could have become motivated to make his contribution to society by serving others. He came to realise that his rise to prominence would have required a great deal of creative effort, and so he tried to utilise all of his talents to achieve it. It would have been important for him not to have assumed that he knew everything that there was to know. He was uninformed about many matters that could have simplified his task. He did believe in himself, however, and when he had decided what he wanted to be, then he would have dedicated himself to becoming the very best. Probably, he would have worked best in direct contact with the public.

But once Gerald knew that he couldn't have afforded to be uninformed, he would have developed well, and have grown successfully in his career. Throughout his life, he should have worked at dispelling errors instilled in his childhood, and this should have given him the urge to pursue a higher education. With this, he could have avoided getting caught in a job situation that was going nowhere. By getting as much formal education as possible, he would not have felt guilty about his lack of knowledge. He was greatly concerned about his resources but if he had learnt to convert his resources into workable skills through education, then he would have had everything he needed to realise his ambitions and goals. Since his learning ability was excellent, this should not have presented a serious problem. Although at times, he had had difficulty in deciding on what action he should have taken to get the most effective results, it was partly because he had lacked sufficient information.

When he had joined with others, who were similarly inclined, he would have found that he had more power at his disposal than he realised, and that his combined effort and energy would have helped him to achieve the important goals required for developing a better integrated, social environment. He may have had more ideas than he had realised for changing prevailing, social values. His most urgent priority then became to make his impressive store of ideas, tangible and real enough, through development and training. He felt guilty about the social injustices that he observed, and he considered himself morally obliged to serve those, who were less capable. But he hadn't to have neglected his own interests, otherwise his generosity would have been abused. He had to have concentrated his attention on people who had the greatest needs. Eventually, he would have tended to stand on his own, but first he had to have grown-up, and have accepted the fact that he had to have earned his independence. If he had implemented his many good ideas, then he should have been able to earn a comfortable income. He could have succeeded as well as others, but he wouldn't have, unless he had been convinced of his objectives. He had to get involved in social issues and environmental problems, and have used these situations as platforms for testing his ideas. His inner and outer Worlds were well co-ordinated, which would have helped him to derive much spiritual satisfaction from his accomplishments. As time went on, he would have become more and more involved, and eventually he would have become dedicated to relieving some of the problems he had observed on the personal, or social, level. His efforts on their behalf would not have gone unnoticed, and helping them, when they couldn't have helped themselves, would have enriched him with much inner satisfaction. Also, he was liable to have met frustration, if he had neglected to consider those, who could have benefitted from his efforts. He would have attracted people who wanted him to indulge them, when they had asked him for help, but he should have avoided letting them take advantage of him. He had the temperamental qualifications for succeeding in his career, especially if he had provided some service to individuals, or to groups. He had to have focused on gaining a foothold in his career, because through his achievements he could have gained the satisfaction, and financial security, that would have been so important for his future life. He would have shown a notable capacity for administration. It might have pleased him to know that when he had served others, he had also served himself, because the chances were that he would have been well-paid. Before long, he would have won the respect of his superiors for his ability to work for their best interests. Because of this, he would have been favoured for promotion, when it had been offered. He had to have been grateful for his privacy, if he had had a low profile in his career. If that career had made sufficient demands on him, and if he had earned a comfortable living from it, then he would have had the best of both Worlds. Providing for his family, should never have become a problem, because he had a variety of skills that he could have turned to, if necessary.

Gerald developed a sense of lack, or of a need, or of a problem to be solved, or of a task to be achieved, in the social and intellectual World around him. He was a self-driving individual, having an executive eccentricity that was neither queerness, nor unbalance, but rather was power. There was a strong, practical capacity, which was neither universal, nor obsessive. He would have been moved more by external factors in his environment than by aspects of his own character.

<u>Vocation:</u> Gerald's sincere concern for people in trouble, or in a precarious, social environment, would have provided an excellent basis for making a worthwhile contribution for improving their circumstances. His career should have involved him working with the public in some way by helping individuals, or groups, deal with social problems. He preferred to carry-out these responsibilities with a certain amount of privacy. In view of his situation, it would have been a good idea to work in an institution for some sort of social program. He could have fulfilled his own needs by using his ability to serve others. Making a contribution that improved the quality of life for others would have allowed him to reach the limits of his potential. For this, he may have had to maintain a low profile in his achievements, but that should have afforded him the privacy to come and go freely, according to the demands of his work. In this way, he would have achieved significance, and have exploited his creativity successfully, if he had used his skills for some cause that would have improved the lives of others.

Gerald's career could have involved him in working with large sums of money. He may have done very well in money management, insurance, stock-brokerage, law, education, medicine, or in personal counselling. People tended to believe that he would always have lived up to their trust. Research and financial consulting comprised two additional fields, in which he could have succeeded, because he would have become stimulated to a high degree of efficiency and excellence. If he had followed this kind of direction, then probably there would have been some incursion into the time he had wanted for personal indulgences. However, the satisfaction that he would have obtained, would have more than compensated him for his loss of pleasure.

Gerald leaned to the Church, and to military life. Moreover, he was suitable for life abroad, and for dealing with foreigners. Furthermore, there would have been success in any of the more profound lines of study. Because he had a talent for dramatizing his ideas, he might have considered writing as a suitable medium for self-expression.

<u>Middle:</u> Although Gerald enjoyed getting an education, respected it and those who are informed, he tended to avoid further education himself, because he had an aversion to purely mental pursuits. He

liked to make money in pleasant ways, e.g. to do with art, beauty, lovely clothes and flowers, and would have been diplomatic and pleasant over money-making, enjoying it for the sake of the lovely things that it brought.

Gerald envied people, who seemed to have the Midas touch. It fascinated him to form alliances with them, and to have watched his financial holdings grow. He enjoyed making investments, and he knew how to keep his business affairs private, until they had developed satisfactorily. He might have benefitted from an investment club, in which members pooled their resources, to buy and sell securities. Financial success and prosperity through increased turnover, were indicated, combined with the power to make money.

Gerald kept his affairs in order because he deplored untidiness. He would have felt more secure and comfortable working from home, or at least, in familiar surroundings. Although he may have been inclined to do the right thing, and to have stayed within the bounds of acceptable practices, he still needed to be alert to deception by those, who would have used him to satisfy their own ends. He knew how to keep the lines of communication open to associates and competitors alike, which gave him an advantage over them. He never stopped looking for ways to implement his ideas, and he took whatever risks were necessary to prove that they worked. He cultivated relationships with socially prominent people and he impressed them with his charming manner and stable temperament. He would have wanted to make a contribution to society and he could have initiated new industrial procedures, or political ideologies. Also, he wanted personal achievements, and personnel changes in his job could have given him that opportunity. But he had to have taken care that he didn't become the victim of such changes. He would not have become satisfied until he had achieved a position of status with its increased benefits.

Gerald tended to fantasise about victories, before he could have proved that he had won. He hadn't to have been content with only moderate gains, for apathy and indulgence are signs of failure. He had to have used his creative imagination to cope effectively with the demands of the real World. He obtained unusual results by working through the conventional, in a sobering of electrical ways, thereby promoting excellent leadership through brilliant ideas. Practical planning and determined self-will united to produce these brilliant results, with some ease of accomplishment, brilliance in management and in unusual, scientific ways. Probably, he became successful in his career, because he had offered better ways to get results. He became a splendid leader in the affairs of the World with vision and readiness to change old ways. However, he did become awkward, if he was not able to be in a position to lead.

Gerald felt compelled, seemingly, to take advantage of opportunities in his life, which he was able to capitalise on, using his latent talents, as a matter of course. This would have involved an element of transformation within himself as well, for example, in his career, from politician to statesman. In this way, he would have become a "glow-worm among worms".

Charity: Early on, Gerald had tried to follow his parents' ideas concerning charity. It wouldn't have been easy for him to express his charitable inclinations, except in ways that wouldn't have offended his parents. He had to have thought for himself regarding charity and yet have maintained close ties with them. His early environment, coupled with his parents' guidance, would have helped him later, when working with charitable affairs. Also, his store of knowledge would have served him well in this regard. Later, through resistance to family, he took opportunities to develop his own charity. Eventually, he would have become responsible for all his own charitable affairs. Here, his keen intuition, imagination and sensitivity would have served him well. His charity was forceful, incisive and enterprising, which made him feel good, and would have helped to soothe his nervous system. Also, his charity was sympathetic and swift in action, rather than through ordered reasoning. It tended to be impractical, but would have been highly receptive to artistic, psychic and benevolent causes. Additionally, it would have involved working with the public in some way, particularly in helping individuals, or groups, with their problems. Unusual ways of charity were preferred. There was some constructiveness in the use of charity for artistic causes. Perhaps, it would have worked better when conducted in hidden, or secluded ways.

Education would have helped Gerald to understand how capable and successful he could have been in his charitable activities. Also, he got help from associates, and learnt from his competitors because they too, could have been catalysts for successful charitable affairs. In addition, he should have listened to his wife's suggestions, who could have been willing to share in his charitable activities. Charity took place in affairs to do with home, domesticity and collecting, and would have been conducted at home. Some domestic power and vitality would have been expressed regarding intangible and secluded charity.

Gerald's mind hay have been stressed by certain, hidden, intangible aspects of his charity. Limitation would have been expressed strongly regarding those aspects. More positively, he didn't mind working for charity without recognition, while he was developing his own creativity for use later in his career. In general, he preferred to fulfil his charitable responsibilities in privacy.

Late: Gerald was gifted with ideas that he would have cultivated for future enrichment. He dreamt that in his later years he would have been free to indulge in all the activities that he had postponed. Being insecure about financial affairs, he dwelt on finding the best way to free himself from material anxiety during his later years. He realised how important it would have been for him to plan for the future. Planning became a high priority, and usually he would have found a way to make the kind of investment that would have assured him of some financial independence in his later years. He would have been happiest in later life, when he had come to understand how to turn his higher mind to more substantial values.

Appearance and Health

Appearance: Although attractive, good-looking and basically enjoying social life, the latter tended to be restrained. Gerald was physically robust, strong and enduring. Above average height, well and proportionately built, he had a spare and slender body. He had an oval face, fresh to ruddy complexion, in a well-formed head, containing evenly developed organs. He had a longish face and neck on a head that tended to be broad at the temples, and somewhat narrower at the chin. His sharp-sighted eyes, which varied from grey to blue, or from hazel to brown, were mounted by bushy eyebrows and roughish hair, varying in colour from dark to sandy. Possibly, he became bald at the temples. Just possibly, his powerful voice was discordant, and he tended to be slow in expression, in speech and in thought, which could have proved depressive.

Health: Gerald had an interest in health and perhaps carried out public work in this area. His mental health varied according to his moods and circumstances. While he was positive and optimistic about life in general, he could have accomplished a great deal. But when his spirits were low, he suffered from all kinds of discomforts because of nervous tension. This tended to play havoc with his digestive system. Although he showed nervous tension, he did have a good, responsive and harmonious nervous system. But mental overstrain could have led to breakdown, followed by irritable temper, in which his incisiveness became satirical and carping. Tension could have snapped, leading to tragedy. But some relief of stress may have been found (a) by thinking about others, and by how much better he was than they (b) by listening to advice from trusted friends and close relatives (c) by improving his level of being informed, and (d) by making plans from the results from all of the previous three.

There was a liability of injuries to his head, or he may have suffered from overwork, excitement, toothache and mouth ulcers. His thighs and buttocks could have become affected. He was apt to suffer from blood disorders, tumours and gout. Inflammatory conditions were possible as a result of measles, small pox, ring worm, neuralgia, vertigo and fevers. His liver, generative and nutritive systems could all have been affected. He had a tendency to falls, chills, orthopaedic troubles, paralysis and accidents. There just may have been some danger from epilepsy, or apoplexy and/or from insanity.

Being anarchical, he may have become obsessed with the possibility of an unfortunate end to his life. The indication was that his death could have been unpleasant.

— —

Figure 3:- Epoch Chart for President Gerald Ford.

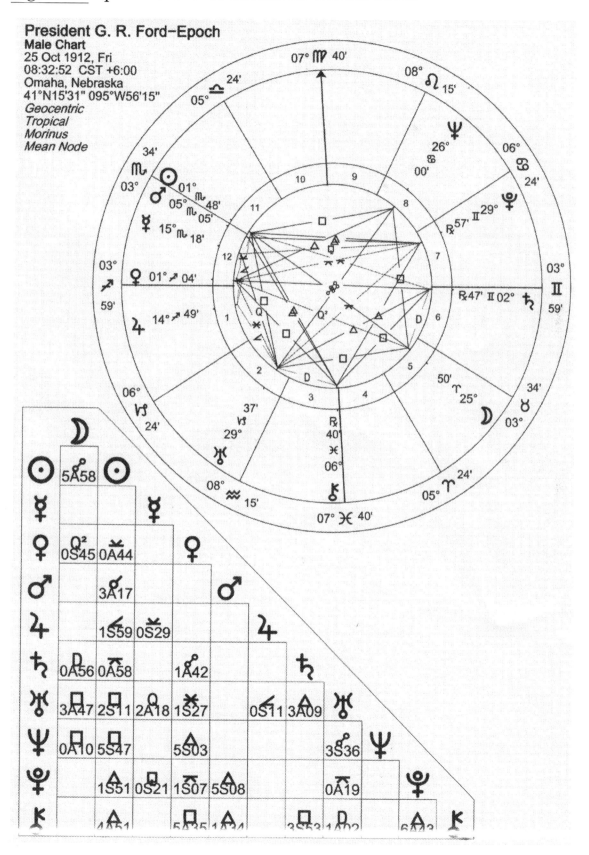

President G. R. Ford—Epoch
Male Chart
25 Oct 1912, Fri
08:32:52 CST +6:00
Omaha, Nebraska
41°N15'31" 095°W56'15"
Geocentric
Tropical
Morinus
Mean Node

Figure 4:- Birth Chart for President Gerald Ford.

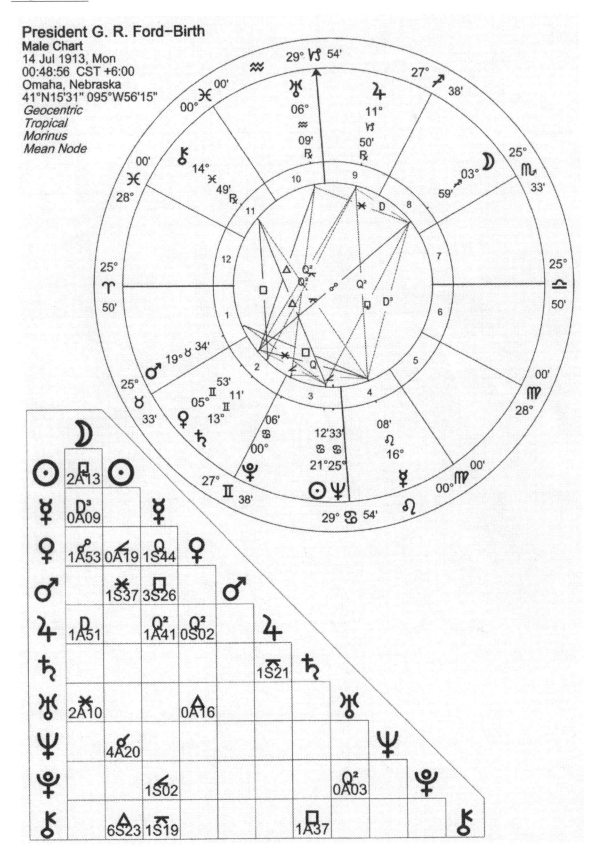

APPENDIX 3

Character Portrait for Oliver Strate

Man, know thyself. Alexander Pope.

Character

<u>General:</u> Courage, enterprise, and the ability to work hard, will be the main attributes of Oliver's personality. There will be some stimulated ambition and the ability to mobilise support, as well as self-confidence, intensified energy, perseverance and endurance. He will be pleasant, smiling and companionable, but he may need to guard against discontent and vacillation. His good character will be affable, courteous, obliging and well-disposed. Happiness, accompanied by a love of peace and beauty, will be indicated mildly. He could become thoroughly expansive in genial, kindly and emotional ways, but also changeful, yet with good intent. His self-expression will be shown energetically through his affections, art and gentle ways, somewhat effeminately, but with good result. He will have a tendency to excellent strength physically and emotionally, which will support his ability to push-on in life. However, control will be needed also, because his results will have to be batted for.

On the other hand, Oliver's self-expression could be limited hurtfully. There will be a tendency for him to be timid through a feeling of personal inadequacy. He may need to guard against tendencies to become stubborn and acquisitive. In addition, there will be a tendencies for him to be explosive, overly aggressive and self-indulgent. These will likely end conditions and force new beginnings, with unhappy results. A related tendency to rash action must be resisted strongly also. Moreover, he will be ready to get rid of the old and begin the new. He may well need to guard against incisiveness and temper that could become satirical and carping. Hardness may have to be endured, which could result in sternness. Altogether, life could become harsh, causing self-pity.

Overall, force and initiative will need to be canalised and ordered, while caution and patience will be enlivened. These results may be depressing to the energetic (like himself) and harmful to the slow and solid. Oliver may develop a vital need for power, independence and supporting mobility, but with softened hot temper, rigidity and relentlessness.

Mentality: Oliver's mind will be practical and sensible, with a mentality that will tend to be active and sensitive. Usually, he will be brilliant, inventive and scientific. He will be fond of study, of intelligent interests and of travel. His speech will be quick and dramatic and his outlook will become independent and self-reliant. He will have good balance, a love of beauty and an interest in the arts. His mind will be improved in so far as charm of speech and pleasantness of manner are concerned. He could become idealistic, contemplative, inspirational, mystical and even conceited.

There will be much good foresight and mental sensitiveness, coupled with humanitarian views and a desire to do good. Results of sensitivity will be likely to be good but vivid imagination may misdirect his mind. Although strong intuitionally, he may need to guard against becoming too much at the mercy of changeful emotions.

Communication will take place in affairs to do with life outside of his home. Oliver will be objective, persistent, efficient, conservative, materialistic and penetrative. His hands can be used cleverly. His mentality and self-expression will both show the traits of harmony and unity. Also, there will be a tendency to self-will, and possibly fanatically so.

Oliver may need to guard against touchiness, involved schemes and acting too much through intuition, rather than from reason. While there may be an extravagance of thought and play, he will need to guard against tension, irritability and disruptive behaviour. There may be some disruptive force with less than happy results. Somewhat explosive conditions can make him seem precipitate, perverted and eccentric, as well as showing blind zeal. Thus, all his good mental points could often become spoilt by a self-centring inclination that may make him appear to be 'dreamy', and one who fails to accomplish that which he regards as ideal. The combination of communication with limitation could have a disastrous result (he mustn't become intimidated by what his father expects of him). Although his limitation may result in a mind lacking width, he may well have great concentration and drive.

Lifestyle: Oliver's urge to acquire dignity, and so become significant within his social environment, will command much of his attention. He will have a strong, almost desperate, desire to become successful among his contemporaries, if only to prove to himself that he is as competent as they are.

He will start with a strong desire to be 'in-command' but then he will keep setting-up competitive situations where, in reality, they may not even exist. He may well not be able to tolerate losing. Possibly, some early life-efforts went un-rewarded and unfulfilled. Later, he will have tried to recapture his past by convincing himself that he does have a degree of power over his life, and over all those, whom he allows to touch him. In fact, there will be a tendency for him to become out-of-tune, as he tries too hard to be himself.

Originally, Oliver will have felt set-off from a definite part of his World, i.e. he will have felt excluded in some subtle way from a complete, half-segment of experience. He will not only have held something, but this something will be placed into a relationship within a larger consideration. His occupied half-segment, containing his planets, reveals his activity and organisation, and this will become his response to the challenge to his existence, presented by the unoccupied half-segment, according to its needs and emptiness. Hence, there will be a marked sense of what he contains, contrasted with what he cannot hold. This will take the form of an advocacy of some cause, or of the furtherance of some mission, or of an introspective concern over the purpose of experience. Always, he will have something to give to his fellows, whether literally or psychologically, whether constructively or vindictively, because his orientation to his World comes from division, i.e. from frustration and uncertainty. The Mercury/Saturn conjunction in Libra, in the 7th House, at Birth, (his leading planet is Mercury) shows how he will try to carry-out his mission (or gain his everyday justification for existence). He will become more self-expanding (or self-seeking) and more practically interested in what things mean and in what they are. He may well prefer to consummate various phases of life, rather than initiate his own experience. As a result, he may well become more idealistic.

Oliver's energy will be expressed with 'heart', strong purpose and creative ability, but he may need to guard against a domineering insistence on becoming over-forceful and hot tempered. He may need to guard against pugnacious bad-temper throughout his life. Also, his energy will be expressed in gay enjoyment of love-making, of children, of games and of all pleasures; all of which harmlessly. Although much may be achieved, his tendency will be to overstrain through over-doing, thereby impairing his vitality. He may even start to develop difficulty in expressing his creativity.

Oliver will have a characteristic and important direction of interest, so that there will be a particular and rather uncompromising direction to his life-effort. There may be some interest in a cause, but much less concern over end-results. Also, he will have no basic desire to conserve either himself, or his resources. Instead, he will be much more likely to adapt his allegiances to lines along which he can make his effort count for the most. At his best, he will become a real instructor and inspirer of others, but at his worst, he may even become an agitator, or malcontent. Either way, he will dip deeply into life, and will pour forth the results of his experiences with unremitting zeal.

More Cerebral Lifestyle material, perhaps for later:

Oliver may tend to withdraw from the creative process and spend much of his time retreating into a dream World that will have become his reality. Much time will be spent searching to reach his inner-being. Often, he will make the mistake of thinking that others can help him to know himself better than he does already. In truth, it will be easy for him to know his inner self, but often it will become so easy that he will attempt to use other factors, thinking that he must seek some great mystery beyond that which he thinks he is capable of understanding. Sometimes, he will be too harsh with himself, and he must learn to judge himself fairly through his higher mind, if he is to become comfortable with his sense of well-being. His life may become very introspective. Still, an inner wisdom, coming from an unseen spiritual guidance, will pervade his entire lifestyle, as soon as he becomes ready to draw upon his inner wealth. Most of the time, his knowledge will lie beyond the words that he can find to communicate all that he knows. However, he will communicate very well on a telepathic level.

He will try to absorb truth from the World around him. He could become deeply spiritual and mystical, but he will not always say what he knows. He will be inclined to spend a great deal of time sorting out the mystery of life, which he senses. He will find many people difficult to comprehend. Although he won't be able to explain how he knows all that he does, he will have a deep instinctual sense of life's true meaning.

He could become highly creative, if he's allowed to do things his own way. One of his biggest problems will be to stop doubting himself. Eastern studies, which can substantiate his sense of non-involvement, could help him to believe in himself more. He will be living through a continuing experience of learning to end self-doubt. Through the use of his higher mind, he should avoid all possible entangling details, which could keep him from the essence of his truth. The inner wealth that he will achieve through life, will be built upon his inner sureness of himself, which, although it will not always appear to mesh with his outer World, will give him an unbounded understanding of his own inner being. This is very progressive, as he will learn ultimately to understand the truth about his earlier life, and so, by extension, the reason for his present life, now.

Thus, Oliver will draw from his awareness and understanding of earlier times, for when he will see the need to use it currently. This particular situation can confirm the occurrence earlier of some sexual abnormality, or homosexuality. Nevertheless, the situation also shows an inner ingenuity that will come through on higher channels of consciousness. These symbolic, major shifts in consciousness, will happen within him. The potential, in this process for real self-growth, will be very great. He will come to know how things work in his outer World, and as a result, he will not always have to experience all of them, in action. His inner mind will be experiencing everything, all the time.

Oliver will prove to be highly adaptable, and will change his opinions, because he will not be possessive of ideas. Also, he won't try to harmonise, disharmonious thoughts continually. He will have a great ability to let the World be, so that in return, it will afford him the inner freedom that he will need. While his changing values will seem, at times, to be quite eccentric, he will nevertheless feel unrestricted by the format of tradition, which keeps most of society bound-up in its own chains. However, with all that he will feel, he will still experience conflict between his Worldly attunement, and his ability to integrate with the rest of his surrounding society. Still, he will have to live in society, but without healthy aspects from Saturn, (which he may not have, at Epoch, but see later). He won't be able to put his Uranian awarenesses into a practical interplay between his knowledge and the World around him.

As Oliver will tend to live on the impractical side, the scope of his imagination will far surpass the reality of the World around him. Highly compassionate, he will often sacrifice much for the needs of others. In addition, he will want to feel needed by his friends, because he will get much deep meaning from them. He will become so deeply appreciative of life itself, that creating things for himself, will become far less important to him than just experiencing the essence of all that he can absorb.

Accordingly, he will bring into his present time, an experience built on earlier dreams. Usually, this will make him idealistic to the point that he will not easily discipline himself to the standards of society. He will always feel that there is a higher music, a more subtle meaning to life and a deeper understanding of what the World calls love. He will become one of a kind, a person who can give generously, not only without expecting anything in return, but also he will not even want the receiver to know that he will have been the giver.

His unusually high level of awareness, coupled with the fact that the traditions and restrictions of society will not bind his creative imagination, means that he will need to learn to balance all that he will feel intuitively, with all that he will have to deal with, on more mundane and practical levels. Thus, it will not be enough for him to imagine something idealistically wonderful; he must find through other areas (in his Birth chart, i.e. 11th House [friends and objectives] →12th [expansion] →10th [career] → 8th [desire and love] → 7th [others in close connection] → [his leading planets Saturn conjoint Mercury in 7th]) to impress his dreams into his own creative reality.

Relationships

Others: Oliver will be stimulated mentally by social contact with others. In fact, social activities will provide him with many opportunities for forming close alliances in endeavours that will allow him to exploit his ideas. His energetic self-expression will tend to be without annoyance to others. He will want to help them, and not offend them, which is admirable. He will overflow with a kindly, humane expression of gently, inspirational ideas and desire to help others.

People will expect a lot from him, and he will be eager to reach out to them, but his early conditioning may have made him too vulnerable emotionally to withstand the difficulties. As an excellent tactician, he will let everybody believe that he shares their views. He will endear himself to others by indicating that he is attracted to people of quality. He will have an intense sense of dominion over other people. His conception of himself will be highly subjective, and based more on his current impulse, than on the way that others reflect back to him. For example: he will insist on his right to assert himself when he gets the impulse. He won't feel that he has to explain his actions to anyone, and he doesn't. He won't take advice, either. Rather, he will become defensive, because he will fear losing the illusion of the position that he has set-up for himself, and so, from time to time, he will create much friction with others. Hence, he could become impatient with those who lack the courage to stand on their own. Only rarely, will he recognise his effect on others. He will come-on too strongly, causing others to back-away from him in fear, as they will be confronted with the weaknesses within themselves. Although he will have a clear perception himself, there will become too much reliance on others, with an inability to move forward spontaneously. He will need to understand his fears and anxieties, so that he can put them into a proper perspective. This will allow him to understand others better, and so come to realise that he is not alone in his fantasies. If any person could have a strong desire to be fair, and yet live selfishly at the same time, then this person will be him.

Friends: Oliver's need for companionship will mean that he will have to make many concessions to others. Generally, he will wait for the other person to make the first move, because he will fear rejection, or a lack of interest.

His friends will be kind, and will be likely to be connected with Neptunian matters, e.g. the intangibles, 'the values', the arts, rhythm, imagination, impressions, the occult and the ideal. He will want to be the first among his friends in everything he does. But the uncertainty of the future, should warn him to use his energy more prudently.

Family: The kind of relationship Oliver had with his parents, will determine whether he will resign himself to the unalterable situations that he will face, or become bitter and resentful. He mustn't become intimidated by what his father expects of him (or by comparison with others' accomplishments) both of which could cause family 'jars'. In these cases, he must remain true to himself.

Oliver will have many plans for his children, and he will hope that they will take advantage of the training that he will have provided, to achieve on their own. Sometimes, there will be difficulty raising a male child, and actually, he could impede the child's progress by expecting too much of him.

Lover: On a sexual level, which will be important to him, Oliver's vibration will alternately attract and repel. But there will be harmonious conditions in his sexual relationships. His ability to enjoy sexual life and all things of beauty, will be robust, but less delicate. Straightaway, there could be trouble with the opposite sex. His love will tend to become more intense, more sexual and more secretive. Jealous emotions and desires will be deep and very strong, prodigal and too passionate. His partnerships will be unconventional, and apt to be broken because of insistence on freedom. There will be a tenseness that may be hard to relax. Thus, partings will be likely through unhappy causes.

Oliver will have a strong desire nature, which he will often express in extreme ways. The unusualness will be apt to be more fascinating and compulsive, but less pleasantly. When the object of his desire will not be available immediately, then he will bide his time patiently, until she/he is, but then he won't accept rejection gracefully.

Oliver's partnerships will be very important to him, but if his partner will not co-operate, then he will forget easily that they had ever existed. His affection will be demonstrative and gay, but he will not want to become enchained. Freedom may well be preferred. Any partnership would bring respon-sibility. His affection could be difficult to express. His partnerships will be subject to disclosures, upheavals and new starts. Thus, there will be some sorrow, or loss through his affections. Temporarily, his life may become solitary.

Although strong, Oliver's sexual drives will not be all-powerful. Often, charm of personality will be a strong element in attracting members of the opposite sex to him. He will want a partner who will support him fully in his goals and will provide him with the strength necessary to pursue them. His partner may well admire his poise and skill in handling people, which will help them both. Also, his partner must share the dedication that he will have set himself, and must continue to support him even if his career intrudes on their relationship. This pre-occupation with his own career may make a dent in his romantic life, and become disturbing to his lover. Consequently, his partner must understand how vulnerable he is, and will come to realise that co-existing careers, in which each will sustain the other, will make for an enduring relationship. Additionally, it will be important for his partner to show that she/he needs him. But he will feel secure in their relationship only if his partner just cannot manage without him. He himself will do anything to make life comfortable and fulfilling for the one he loves.

Oliver will have a compelling need to become involved with persons who will share his strong desire for warm, sociable relationships. Usually, he will be on his best behaviour, which he will consider to be a good investment to win someone who attracts him. He will make many concessions when he wants attention from someone he desires for a close relationship, and he will let that person's needs take precedence over his own. Probably, his partner will become the source of his inspiration for continually progressing to higher levels in his career. Although he will need this urging, he will also feel that he will be free to exploit his potential in his own way.

Yet there will remain some feeling of inadequacy concerning matters of others in close connection. He may well choose a partner whose ego drive matches his own. He may marry a foreigner, or live abroad after marriage, or may go into such partnership for business, or profession. Additionally, he might marry for financial gain, or simply because he will not like living alone, which are not the best reasons for doing so. It would be better if he married when he will feel that he has met his ideal mate.

Oliver may well assume that his partner will be fascinated by his forceful nature, which may be so, but probably his desire to please, and to provide all of life's necessities, will be even more attractive. His partner will become more and more appreciative of his continuing efforts to enrich and sustain their relationship. He will do almost anything for the one he loves, and the resulting happiness will be all the thanks that he needs. A successful marriage is indicated.

Career

Oliver's destiny will lie mainly in his own hands, rather than in the hands of others (from his Epoch chart) and largely in the hands of others (from his Birth chart) either through marriage, partnership, or general association. His fate will be marked, and his life most eventful, but his rise and fall, honour and degradation, will depend very considerably on the position of the Sun (at Epoch) in Capricorn, in the 10th House, and on its aspects, specifically on its sesqui-quadrate to Mars (chart ruler, in Leo, in the 5th House) but also on its strong square to Saturn (Sun-ruler, exalted in Libra in the 7th House, but malaspected). There will be success in things of the sea, in businesses to do with oil and liquids, and with art, acting, psychism, and in hidden ways, especially if concerned with philanthropic work. There will be gain through his partner's money, inherited money and/or possessions. On the other hand, there will be loss through impulse, speculative investment and risky enterprises.

<u>Early:</u> Oliver will show much ambition, a keen desire to be at the head of everything, extreme independence, self-assertion and egotistical tendencies. There will be little that Oliver could not accomplish when his feelings and will-to-achieve are brought together, under control, through self-discipline. Tough roads require a superior vehicle, and he has such a one, but he will need to understand its potential and its limitations. Dealing with frustration will give him the determination to withstand further conflicts, and conflict will stimulate him to use his creativity when solving his problems. Eventually, he will rise to prominence and have the authority to motivate others to support him with his objectives, while realising theirs. The public will be quick to approve of, or dismiss him, so that he must prepare himself for the abrasive situations that he will encounter. Importantly, he should establish some defence against these emotionally painful abrasions, or his effectiveness will become diminished considerably.

Oliver's strong desire for recognition will impel him to seek a career in which he will be able to pursue his objectives in his own way. He will find satisfaction in a responsible position, in which others must rely on his good judgement and expertise. Developing his creativity would help to raise his credibility. Oliver will underestimate his ability and talent to make an important contribution to society, and may well let others gain the advantage over him. But with good training, he could learn to appreciate his creative gifts, which in turn, will allow him to succeed in professional (and personal) relationships. If he will establish his goals, and develop his creativity, then these will give him the strength, courage and determination to succeed. Also, as he will have a notable capacity for administration, then there will be a strong possibility that he will achieve success early in life.

Oliver's goals could be so high that he will want to reach complete fulfilment in everything he undertakes. He must come to realise how unrealistic these expectations are, in his daily life. Probably because he will choose a public career, he will have to remember his obligations to those, who will be affected by his actions. There will be ambition to lead; he will always be in the front, and he will not seldom be in the way. He will be difficult to deal with; he will be always starting new things, but rarely finishing them.

Most of his opportunities will result from contacts with friends, associates and fellow workers, and he will resent it when his attempts to create the conditions he wants, don't work-out as planned. Although he will want fervently the privilege of determining his own fate in every way, he will realise that to have that luxury, he must have to depend on circumstances and opportunities provided by others, which will be contradictory. His striving for significance will mean that he must depend on others for opportunities. Importantly, he will need to adjust to this situation, and proceed from there.

Oliver will derive the greatest benefit by working closely with people over whom he has some authority. Life will tend to be rigorous, or hard, but lessons of duty and self-control will be learnt. To help here, he does have some ability to work hard and to push-on in life. Oliver will become extremely sensitive to human frailty, but will come to know how to solve the problems it causes. He will develop a tendency that he should look for a career with a future, so that the investment that he will have made, and will continue to make, will yield enduring possibilities for growth and the expansion of his services.

Although at times, it may be painful for him to have to accept the limitations imposed by society, he will have decided to help others, and will need to have greater self-determination, despite the persistence of his anxieties about restricted freedom. His sensitiveness to the needs of those around him, will be an indication of his considerable potential for growth and development. He will have the ability to make worthwhile contributions to help to relieve many social problems. He should begin to focus on his destiny by helping those who are close to him. Also, it will become extremely important for him to define his goals and objectives and to understand that he will have the resources necessary to realise them. These resources will help people to find their way out of the 'darkness of ignorance'. Knowing that someone will be depending on him, will stimulate him to extend himself on his/her behalf. He will know how to arouse people to use their own resources, so that they can sustain themselves without him. Having people satisfy his physical needs, should not become a condition of his help. His complete awareness of society's problems will carry a responsibility that he will be unable to ignore. Also, the tendency will be that an important feature of his destiny will be his sharing of his talents with those who will need to be informed. He will have the ability to arouse people to support him in his endeavours, which in time, will prove beneficial to them as well.

Oliver may have to guard against over-imagination leading to a lack of common-sense in everyday affairs, and to becoming too easily emotional, leading to exaggerative expression. But some of his objectives in life will be inspired by 'hunches', which usually will be right. In the attempt to reach his goals, frequently he will become disappointed, so that he will have to redefine them periodically. However, unless he chooses to work to improve the quality of life for those around him, he won't ever feel fully content with his achievements.

Vocation: Oliver will be suitable for the army, for engineering, or mining, or for large business undertakings, or for public life. He could prove suitable for literary pursuits, for philosophical and/or scientific occupations, having an intellect keenly critical, but not destructively so. As he will not be devotional in any way, he will bring everything to the test of practical life in outward action. However, some harshness, or hardness, irritability and/or a lack of self-discipline, could cause public conflict.

There may be many fields that he could choose from, for his vocation, but he should become equipped to handle authority, because very likely, he will have a position of it. Management, counselling, law and social services comprise some of the areas wherein he could find suitable expression. He would rise early to prominence in government service, politics, industry and public relations. Business and all public life will attract him. He will have a deep sense of obligation to the victims of political, social, or economic injustice. He will feel that he has an important mission to help those who cannot help themselves. He will become qualified for a career that will involve helping to solve the problems of society, thereby enriching the lives of those, who truly need assistance. His future will depend on how well he can satisfy these social obligations. His success in handling broad, social issues will result from his uncanny ability to understand people's needs.

Oliver may have an interest in psychic matters, and have a readiness to work for research in such ways. Surgery and psychology will attract his mind. As a writer, or speaker, he will benefit from balance, but ease rather than strength would be gained (which could well suit Oliver, here). Kindly, emotional ways could prove helpful for the arts, and for psychic work. He may well develop an intense love of music.

<u>Middle:</u> There may be a loss of power and prestige, as well as unforeseen twists in Oliver's career. Always on his mind, will have been the fear that he might not have lived up to the public's expectations. And so, he will always feel some apprehension about his ability to carry-out his plans as defined originally, although the public may never become aware of his secret anxiety. His concept of progress will represent frustration, as he will constantly feel that he should be doing something other than what he is doing. He will experience reviewing his entire creative process because much of that which he has created previously, has only brought him discontent. He will tend to mull-over his setbacks in life, rather than reach ahead for new horizons. Additionally, he will find it difficult to sacrifice any of his desires, but some sacrifice will be necessary as an investment in order to achieve the long-range goals that he will have set for himself. Sometimes, he will feel that he is battling against the tide, but he will also attempt to create those currents, so that he will have something to swim against. Moreover, his tendency will be to avoid activities that would take him away from the main stream, where everyone else is. Furthermore, his uncontrolled outbursts could put him out of commission, so that he will need to conserve his energy. He will need to plan to work more efficiently. He might become obsessed with a compelling need to achieve self-discipline. He might even become an island unto himself.

Instead, he will have to learn what will become truly valuable to him, in terms of his feelings and well-being. He will be able to do this best when he overcomes his unconscious feelings of superiority, which have been feeding his ego, rather than building-up his confidence. But he will have to remain sensitive to his associates' needs.

There will be success through foreign countries, and with people from abroad, but there could be difficulties here also. The chances are that he will more than compensate for any subtle fears about his qualifications. In this regard, he should become reassured by his superiors' approval of his effectiveness. He will become a capable executive, having a strong will, much force of character, coupled with an ability to work hard, thereby accomplishing much. Also he knows that money can accomplish much, especially in the direction of his life achievement. He will hope that he can be of service to people who can't help themselves. There may well become a necessity for him to deal with finances for others. In addition, people will sense that he is concerned with their problems. He will be brought into prominence, especially in governmental affairs, or where there is great responsibility. Usually, he will remember each person who has helped him earlier, so that he can reciprocate when this becomes possible.

Charity: Oliver's mind and mental outlook will be improved by contact with charitable affairs. His imagination will be fertile with regard to humanitarian/scientific charitable concerns. But his charitable activities could cause him to overstrain, through overdoing.

Late: Oliver will become deeply concerned about fulfilling his ambitions, and about achieving security for his retirement. This will be the reason why he will have wanted a career with growth potential, so that he could make as many gains as possible. Greater efficiency with work will have helped to prevent him from becoming burned-out by exhaustion before his later years. Knowing that he will have made an important contribution to serving people's needs, will enrich his later years with contentment. If his life energies will tend more towards spiritual, rather than physical, pleasures, then these will become a source of joy and happiness.

Appearance and Health

Appearance: Oliver will tend to be thin, of medium height, somewhat slightly built, active, mobile and changeable. He will have light hair and bright, magnetic eyes. His manner will appear cool and cautious, so that he will seem more limited than he is really.

Health: Oliver will have good health and an harmoniously-working, nervous system. Possibly, his head may be liable to suffer, and he may be affected by, for example, toothache, neuralgia, gumboils, small pox, ringworm and vertigo. Later, he may become susceptible to dropsy complaints and to chronic irregularities of his system. His nervous system may suffer, e.g. explosiveness and emotional strain may result in nervous stress, and just possibly, paralysis. Additionally, he may become prone to minor accidents, such as falls, chills and orthopaedic troubles. In these cases, he will need to guard against overstrain and tension.

An easy death is indicated for him.

— — — — — — — — — — — — — — — — — — —

Figure 5:- Epoch Chart for Oliver Strate.

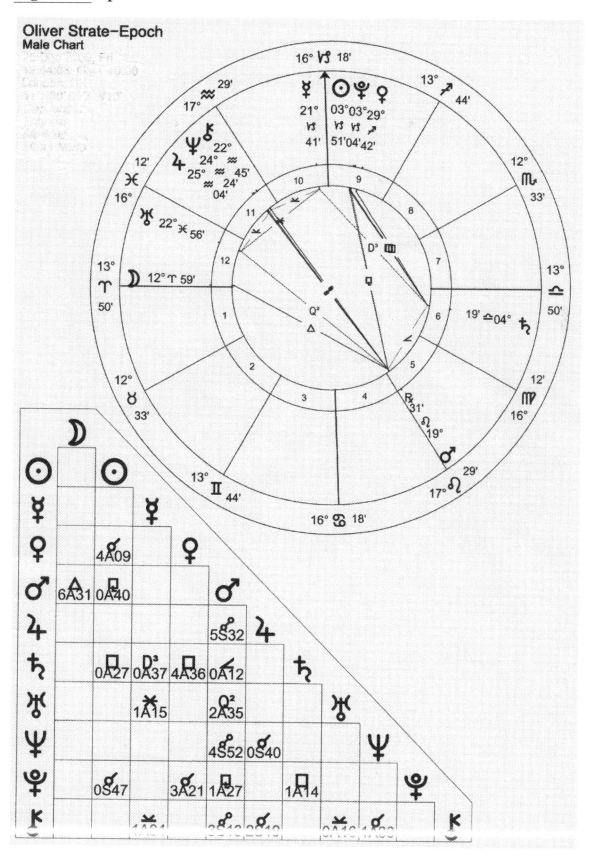

Figure 6:- Birth Chart for Oliver Strate.

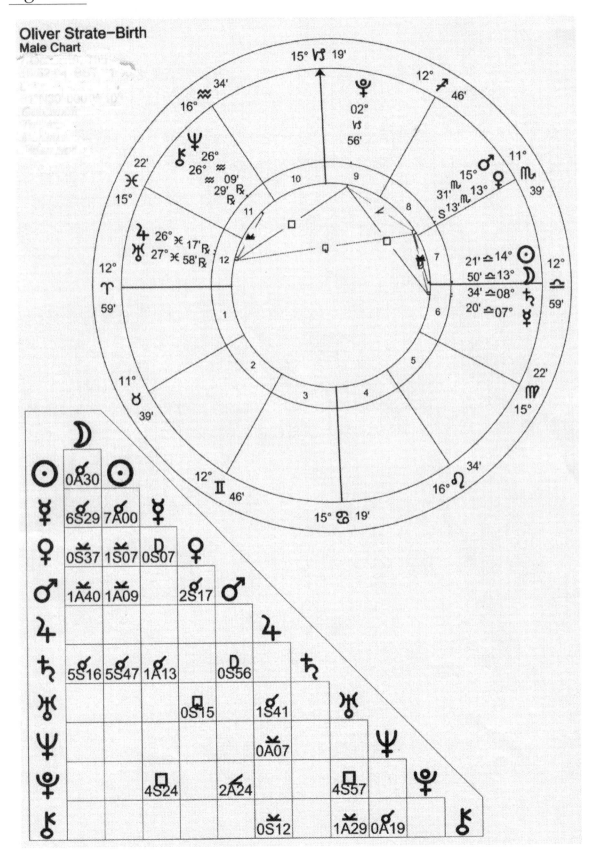

Printed in the United States
By Bookmasters